USE ♦ THE ONLY ORIGINAL CHICKEN HOUSE ON THE FAIR GROUNDS, TREASURE ISLAND, . . . SAN FRANCISCO, CALIFORNIA

DROP IN
FOR
HOT COFFEE
BARBECUED SANDWICH 15¢
STEAK SANDWICH 20¢
HAMBURGER
SIZE

HOOT HOOT
I SCREAM
1201

Jim Heimann

# CALIFORNIA CRAZY

American Pop Architecture

TASCHEN

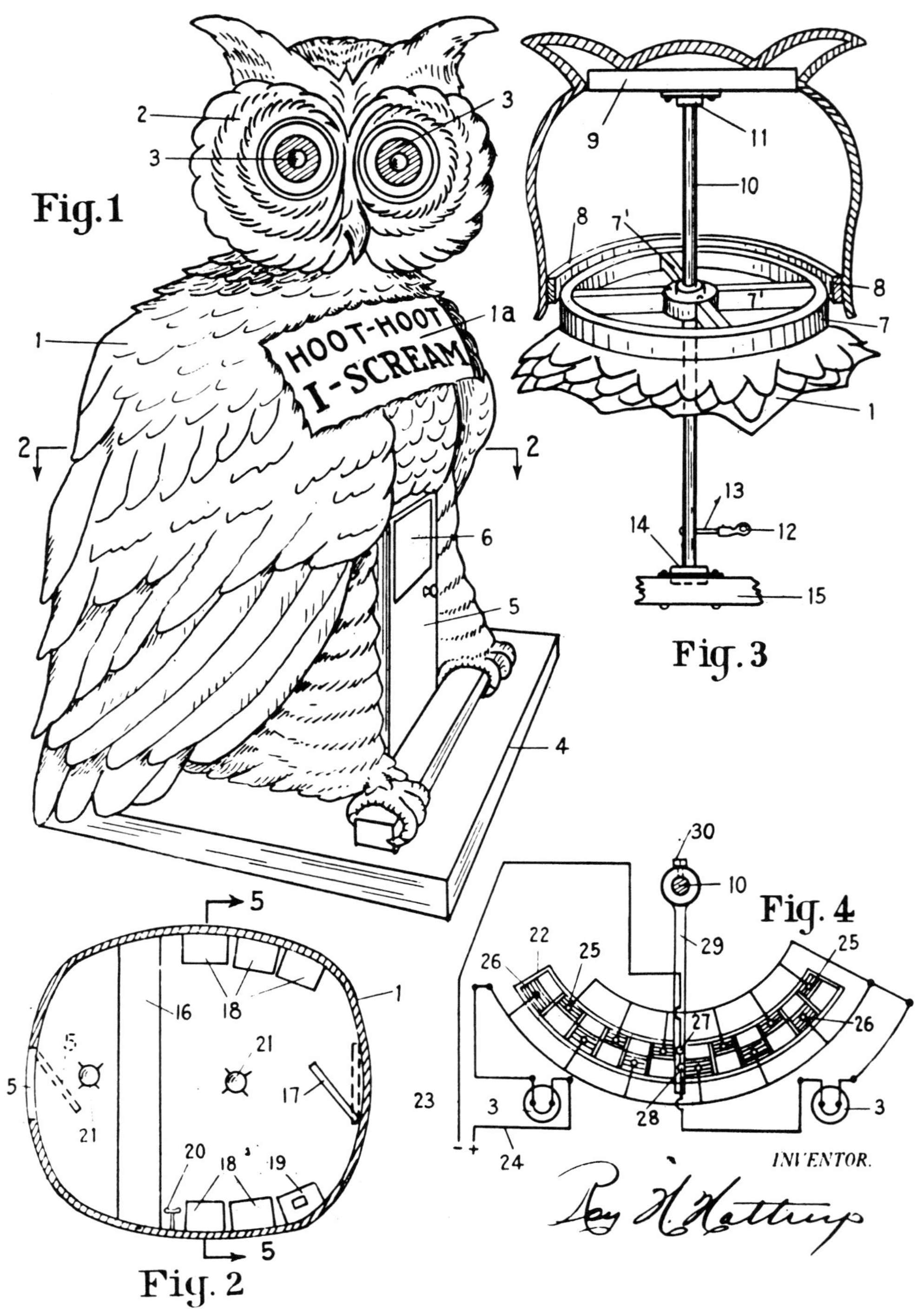
Fig. 1
HOOT-HOOT
I-SCREAM
Fig. 3
Fig. 2
Fig. 4
INVENTOR.

# Contents

# What Makes California Crazy

by Jim Heimann

Many of the world's major metropolises lay claim to some outstanding feature that sets them apart. Los Angeles, a latecomer among the world's major cities, developed after nearly all of the international capitals were well established. Significantly, it also developed in the age of the automobile. Thus it became, by default, the only city to develop around the needs and possibilities of the car. What Los Angeles lacked in history it made up for with space—a wide geographic area devoid of development—and an optimistic attitude that anything was possible.

In the first part of the 20th century, California, particularly the Southland, traded in agriculture, oil, aviation, and fantasy. Prodded by the movie-making business in Hollywood and surrounding communities, one industry that made a distinct impact on the landscape was that of motion pictures. Add a freethinking populace fueled with a healthy dose of boosterism and a desire to leave the past and reinvent itself, and a climate was created that served as a perfect incubator for the outrageous and amazing. If you wanted to make a peculiar display or sign for your business it was more apt to be accepted in Southern California than in places that placed higher value on conformity and fitting in. It was this atmosphere that made possible the making of a giant flowerpot or a roadside café in the shape of a pig. California was not only ripe for programmatic architecture but provided a template that emboldened people in other states and countries to thumb their noses at the status quo and build the impossible—or at least the highly improbable.

PAGE 1
Coffee Cup, 8901 West Pico Boulevard, Los Angeles, ca. 1929

PAGES 2-3
Cabazon Dinosaurs, ca. 1993. Designer: Claude Bell

PAGE 4
Hoot Hoot I Scream, 1201 Valley Boulevard, San Gabriel, 1932. Owner: Tillie Hattrup

PAGE 6
Hoot Hoot I Scream patent drawings, ca. 1930

OPPOSITE
J. W. Robinson Company, Los Angeles, 1929

J.W. ROBINSON CO.

SANTA CLAUS
WILL BE HERE AT
7 P.M. SATURDAY
VAN FLEET & DURKEE No 176
DuBarry

BELMONT

PREVIOUS SPREAD
Santa Claus display at Shell Oil station, Los Angeles, 1930

LEFT
Enoch Chevrolet, 8730 Long Beach Boulevard, South Gate, ca. 1939

BELOW
Vogue Tyres billboard, Los Angeles, 1935

TOP
United States Tires billboard, Needles, ca. 1937

BOTTOM
Adohr Farms Milk statue, Los Angeles, ca. 1928

LEFT
Currie's Ice Cream, ca. 1938

BELOW
Safe Spot, Los Angeles, 1933

OPPOSITE
Promotional stunt, Los Angeles, ca. 1928

HERE
GASOLINE
10
HOLLYWOOD LAUNDRY CO.
open
ALL
NIGHT
CHOP SUEY
SIGNS
Show Cards
TAILORS
SIGNS

Experts
Leimert Business Center
PARK
VIEW PARK
BUILT UP SECTION
Leimert Business Center
Another Vine and Hollywood in the making

OPPOSITE
Giant arrow at Leimert Business Center, Los Angeles, 1928

RIGHT
Tower service station, Beverly Boulevard, Los Angeles, ca. 1940

BELOW
Midwick View Estates opening, Monterey Park, 1930

FOLLOWING SPREAD
Auto Show, Wilshire Boulevard, Los Angeles, 1935

Demand
GOLDEN WEDDING
Schenley PRODUCT . . . LOOK FOR THE MARK OF

CHILI
HOT DOGS
and
HAMBURGERS
OPEN

# California Crazy Redux

by Jim Heimann

It has been almost 40 years since the first edition of *California Crazy* was published. The modest little book that sought to shed light on an obscure footnote to architectural history has become, over time, a catalyst for studied interest in roadside architecture, a textbook for architecture courses, and a passion for a subculture of those who love oddball buildings. In the intervening years, public recognition of these types of buildings has not only increased, but has inspired a limited resurgence of the style for which the book coined the term *programmatic architecture*. Thanks to this revival many new images have surfaced throughout the world, revealing yet another layer of this architectural style and acknowledging that contemporary and vintage examples of programmatic architecture can be found throughout the United States and other countries.

*California Crazy* maintains the pursuit of vernacular roadside architecture—aided, of course, by countless collectors, institutions, and chroniclers of these types of images. The discovery of more images of unusual buildings has further substantiated the idea that Southern California was indeed the locus of this architectural subcategory. The original edition of this book noted that the media had focused on a dozen or so buildings and underestimated the actual number that existed. In fact, dozens more of these structures were built. Los Angeles's physical being also contributed to the confusion. These buildings were spread across the city's geographic range of over 450 square miles, which diluted their effect. Although these types of buildings did not literally line the streets, no other metropolitan area could match their numbers.

Research in the past decade or so has revealed several new aspects to the story of offbeat architecture. The addition of pictorial essays in this book serves to give further insight into the nascent period of these buildings in contained amusement environments as well as to consider the role of Southern California's sprawling landscape as an incubator for this building type to flourish. This book also includes oversized advertising signs and statues as an adjunct to the architectural examples — an extension of the California Crazy concept. Residential architecture,

PAGE 20
Pup Café, 12732 West Washington Boulevard, Culver City, ca. 1934

BELOW
Hollywoodland, ca. 1923

OPPOSITE
*Collier's* article, April 6, 1929

marginally included here, is used as a point of reference to show how commercial and private architecture influenced each other. Overall, these inclusions reinforce that Los Angeles was, and is, a rather unusual place in comparison to the rest of the world—one in which the propagation of the eccentric and nonconforming is cultivated and appreciated.

While this book focuses on California, it is important to note that contemporary examples of this architectural type continue to flourish and be embraced throughout the world, continuing this eccentric tradition. Keep your eyes open. *California Crazy* continues to express the spirit of nonconformity in a sometimes very confined architectural world.

The Igloo with its polar bear and ice-locked vessel is almost chill enough in its exterior to serve the purpose for which its wares are intended. It's an ice-cream parlor—as if you wouldn't know!

*All photos by Brown Bros.*

You hear plenty enough about ham-trees, what with the popularity of all-colored revues and all, but here's an actual one—advertising a mart across the street

Just a little trinket to keep you from forgetting where the gift shop is

Toot-toot! One railroad crossing you may race over in safety—unless it's a bit of a meal you're in search of. In which case, it's an invitation to stop, look and eat

This one required many a conference of great minds before "Health Triumphant" emerged to boost interest in a prescription pharmacy. And we've seen worse in more enduring stone in some of our public parks

WHY?
COFFEE PARLOR
WE SERVE TREE TEA ONLY
WE USE M-J-B COFFEE WHY?
M·J·B
WHY?
M·J·B
WHY?
LOOK! ARE YOU A SHOT?
TRY FOR
CASH PRIZES

# From Amusement Zones to the Road

by Jim Heimann

The focus on roadside architecture has always been on the automobile and the ever-expanding highways and byways of America in the early 20th century. What has been previously bypassed was the development of fantastic architecture that was created for entertainment purposes in contained environments, such as expositions, world's fairs, and amusement parks. Unlike roadside architecture, which aimed to attract customers on the road via the unusual and unexpected, architecture in these contained environments relied on the pedestrian and was for the most part an exercise in entertaining visitors by offering them something they couldn't find elsewhere. Built primarily as facades in the amusement zones of these fairs and expositions, these predecessors of roadside programmatic architecture were constructed and developed (and, in some ways, copied) for the auto trade as freestanding structures.

The Panama-Pacific International Exposition (or PPIE) of 1915, held in San Francisco, was not the first expo or amusement zone to include unusual architecture. Examples abound from the Pan-American Exposition of 1901 in Buffalo, New York, to the Louisiana Purchase Exposition of 1904 in St. Louis, Missouri, to the 1910 amusement zones of Venice and Ocean Park, California. The "Fun Zone" at the PPIE was a showcase of whimsical structures that would clearly influence many of the oddball buildings that would be built in the forthcoming decade. The attraction "Captain, the Educated Horse" had a two-story stucco horse as an entry. Farther along the midway, a gigantic Uncle Sam bent over fairgoers while holding the fob to a giant watch that dangled over the Souvenir Watch Palace. A 120-foot gilded Buddha dominated the Japan Beautiful Pavilion, while three-story ostriches served as portals to the Ostrich Farm. The enormous Bowls of Joy were replicas of roly-poly toys that dwarfed the patrons standing in line for one of the exposition's more dangerous thrill rides. Oversized

PAGE 24
Why? Coffee Parlor, Pan-Pacific International Exposition, San Francisco, 1915

LEFT
Gillette Safety Razor Co. exhibit, Pan-Pacific International Exposition, San Francisco, 1915

OPPOSITE
Souvenir Watch Palace, Pan-Pacific International Exposition, San Francisco, 1915

jack-in-the-boxes, colossal elephant heads, huge sculpted angels, and super-scaled telephones and typewriters could be found scattered throughout the Fun Zone and exposition pavilions. A fantasy secure behind their walls, the buildings nonetheless drew throngs to the amusement zone and made a lasting impact on the public. These facades would become a key visual language to a broader audience once outside the confines of an enclosed environment.

What also set PPIE's Fun Zone apart from its predecessors were developments in construction methods and materials, which allowed for more refined versions of mimetic architecture. Improved stucco technology along with seven varieties of finishing material developed especially for the fair made the shaping of aberrant buildings and facades more sophisticated and malleable. In addition, craftsmen with superlative skills for plasterwork and painting made a distinctive leap in what could be realized with novelty construction.

Another important aspect of the PPIE was the appearance of director D. W. Griffith from Hollywood. In San Francisco for the Motion Picture Exhibitors Association conference, he was invited to speak at the exposition. He quickly took note of the building techniques and eventually hired PPIE workers to come to Los Angeles and help construct and paint the massive set of Babylonia for his production of *Intolerance*. Devoid of fences and positioned on the streets of Hollywood for all to see, the set became an instant landmark and set the tone for the intrusion of Hollywood fantasy on the urban landscape. In this way the whimsical programmatic architecture made its transition from exposition to Hollywood studio, and ultimately to the California roadside. As local proprietors looked for workers to construct their buildings, many of them found that set builders had the skills to create their fantastic roadside ventures. Thus Hollywood could effectively be held responsible for influencing the Southland's preponderance

JAPAN
JAPAN
JAPAN

OPPOSITE
Japan Beautiful, Pan-Pacific International Exposition, San Francisco, 1915

BELOW
Pan-Pacific International Exposition, San Francisco, 1915

of this building type. A byproduct of these movie studio construction methods and building materials was their temporary nature that would partially contribute to their eventual demise.

The PPIE set in motion for California to be the locus of programmatic architecture. The Hollywood connection, the sprawling geography, and the culture of the automobile propelled this architectural type to prosper and flourish there—making California a bit more crazy than the rest of the world.

BOWLS OF JOY
10¢ SOUVENIR 10¢
OF THE EXPOSITION
10¢

BOWLS OF JOY
H.L. JUDELL & CO
SMOKE SHOP
CHANCELLOR C

CAWSTON OSTRICH FARM
100 Ostriches On
EXHIBITION
ADMISSION 10¢ TO FARM
ENTRANCE.
100 LIVE ONES IN THE FARM.
100 LIVE ONES IN THE FARM.
ENTRANCE TO SALESROOM FREE
EXHIBITION
PAY A VISIT
VISIT
OSTRICH FARM
SALES ROOM
FREE Admission

PREVIOUS SPREAD
Bowls of Joy, Pan-Pacific International Exposition, San Francisco, 1915

OPPOSITE
Cawston Ostrich Farm, Pan-Pacific International Exposition, San Francisco, 1915

THIS PAGE
Captain, the Educated Horse (before and after), Pan-Pacific International Exposition, San Francisco, 1915

WONDER
SUBMARINES
TOYLAND
SCENIC

OPPOSITE
Toyland, Pan-Pacific International Exposition, San Francisco, 1915

BELOW
Creation of the World, Pan-Pacific International Exposition, San Francisco, 1915

LEFT
The Submarines, Pan-Pacific International Exposition, San Francisco, 1915

BELOW
Scenic Railway, Pan-Pacific International Exposition, San Francisco, 1915

OPPOSITE
African Dip, Pan-Pacific International Exposition, San Francisco, 1915

Orange Blossom Candies
AFRICAN DIP

TEHUANTEPEC

OPPOSITE
Tehuantepec, Pan-Pacific International Exposition, San Francisco, 1915

THIS PAGE
*Intolerance* set, Sunset and Hollywood Boulevards, Los Angeles, 1916

OPEN
ICHES 10¢
ORANGE JUICE
MILK

# A Century of California Crazy

by Jim Heimann

California has never lacked superlatives. The Golden State's claim as host to the largest concentration of bizarre and odd-shaped buildings is just another feather in the cap of a state whose reputation was built on towns that called themselves the "artichoke capital of the world" or "home to the world's largest chinchilla farm." While Southern California contained a large number of offbeat buildings, the rest of the state enjoyed a healthy sampling of architectural anomalies as well. Given the free-wheeling nature of California, its perceived lack of history, wealth of affordable land, and anything-goes attitude, it is easy to see why the state and climate were perfect for embracing these buildings.

Reinforced by chamber of commerce boosters, railroad companies, and real estate promoters, California quickly transformed itself by a series of land booms in the latter part of the 19th century that continued through to the first part of the 20th. These land booms brought the state a tremendous influx of new arrivals, who borrowed or brought their architectural heritages with them. The lack of an architectural tradition and the motivation by transplants to the Golden State to start fresh and experiment brought an eclectic vision to the area. Before the automobile became a fixture on the landscape and accelerated the construction of roadside architecture, Californians were treated to a more sedate assortment of architectural aberrations. Various revivals of historic periods were popular in commercial ventures, especially when the Mission Style became fashionable in the 1880s. Transit stations, stores, and schools borrowed elements of a romantic mission past, reinforcing once again the illusion of a California that never was. In the early part of the 20th century, the Arts and Crafts movement provided a touch of Asian flavor. Craftsman bungalows featured the best examples of this influence and the pagoda-like homes that lined many a new suburban tract were a striking contrast to the California landscape.

PAGE 40
Betsy Ann Ice Cream and Candy, Los Angeles, ca. 1928

LEFT
Fish stand, Venice Pier, ca. 1910

OPPOSITE
The Yelps, Venice Amusement Zone, ca. 1916

During this same time period in Southern California, where no tradition impeded them, developers experimented with a variety of architectural styles. In 1912, the *Los Angeles Times* made note of this experimental climate in describing the construction of a downtown apartment building that claimed to be the first to adapt early Aztec architecture to modern structural designing:

*"Los Angeles is noted for the diversity of architecture entering the planning of its buildings, the types of design here being almost as cosmopolitan as the population. Every type of architecture prevailing in the Mediterranean countries of Europe has been copied and adapted. The Englishman has brought here the sturdy lines of the British buildings. The chateau in its many forms has suited the ideas of many. The charming Swiss chalet has been modified to suit local requirements and has become one of the most popular of all styles. The Mission, California's own architecture, is to be encountered at every turn. The bungalow has retaken on an individuality and charm that has won for the Southland types a worldwide reputation. Every Eastern American type has been introduced here."*

*"That the architecture of the prehistoric civilizations of North America has never been copied by the builders has occasioned comment at times from foreign visitors to this country. In Mexico and Central America especially the races found by the first white conqueror had developed not only a high degree of structural ingenuity, but a real sense of the artistic. It may be urged in their favor, too, that they were not copying from any classics of still more ancient days as were Europeans of the same period, and that their work was truly original."*

When Abbot Kinney created his visionary development of Venice, California,

CLIMBING
THE
YELPS
ADMISSION
10¢

between 1904 and 1906 on the marshlands of suburban Los Angeles, he was part of a pioneering effort that transformed Southern California from a vast agricultural plain to a land of fantasy and illusion. By importing the imagery of Venice, Italy, for a cultural center and seaside resort, he helped set the tone for a free-spirited architectural atmosphere. Principal buildings of the resort followed Venetian lines while other attractions infused the area with the exotic. Gondolas glided along a grid of canals, camels paraded the streets giving visitors rides, and an early midway contained reproductions of the streets of Cairo and Tokyo. The Ship Café (1905) was one of the earliest of the faux buildings constructed on the Venice Pier. Built on the side of the wharf extending over the ocean, it gave the illusion of resting on the water when in fact no part actually touched the ocean. The Ship Café's popularity reigned for several decades and peaked when the early Hollywood movie colony frequented it as a Prohibition hangout.

In a Venice amusement park that evolved out of the resort several years later, many buildings featured facades of fantastic proportions. Spilling out of the amusement zone and onto the boardwalk was the Venice Scenic Railway (1910), which was encased in a stucco mountain range with oversized deer clinging to the precipices. In the adjacent amusement zones of Ocean Park, massive stucco monsters flanked a thrill ride called Dragon Gorge (1911), a mountain rose from the Grand Canyon Scenic Railway (1911), and the Ocean Park bathhouse (1905) on the boardwalk was a maze of minarets and onion domes. For visitors as well as local residents, it was a giddy architectural fantasy come true and another affirmation of California's animated architecture.

As an architectural bridge, Venice provided the subtle inspiration for things to come. As the automobile gained momentum in the pre–World War I era, an eclectic mix of architectural styles continued to pop up along the roadside and in urban

OPPOSITE
Shrine Auditorium, 665 West Jefferson Boulevard, Los Angeles, ca. 1920
RIGHT
Theosophical Institute, Point Loma, ca. 1905

areas. These structures presaged more impossible structures to come, and most were replications of historical styles. These period revivals were often adaptations of European, Spanish, or Mediterranean architecture. For example, the Shrine Auditorium (1920–26) near downtown Los Angeles employed the exotic imagery of the Middle East in one of its first auditoriums. In San Diego, the Old Log Cabin (1911), an early roadside refreshment stand, played with the idea of a rustic frontier past complete with an interior that exuded a pioneer atmosphere while dispensing soft drinks. The large Los Baños bathhouse in downtown San Diego was constructed in flamboyant Mission Style, while in nearby La Jolla, Anna Held, an eccentric and free-spirited artist, created an ark-shaped home as part of the Green Dragon Colony, an early 20th century collection of cottages on the side of a hill. In Point Loma, across the San Diego Bay, an emerging utopian commune, the Theosophists, constructed a Greek temple overlooking the ocean as well as a series of quasi-Asian buildings topped with onion-shaped domes of purple and aquamarine glass. Leslie Brand, a financier and a developer of Glendale, a Los Angeles suburb, created a mansion he named El Miradero (1902–04) on one thousand acres of prime foothill land. Saracenic in style, it was inspired by the East Indian Pavilion of the 1893 Columbian Exposition in Chicago.

While many of these types of architectural styles and amusement parks were not exclusive to California, their confluence and impact in an emerging landscape was its striking contrast to companion structures and amusement zones in the other parts of the United States. It was becoming clear that California was slowly becoming crazier.

Hollywood, which was to become a magnet for architectural illusions, further enhanced its reputation for offbeat architecture even before the movies arrived. Real estate developer and retired doctor

BELOW
Bernheimer residence, 1999 Sycamore Avenue, Hollywood, ca. 1911

OPPOSITE
Glengarry Castle, Argyle and Franklin Avenues, Hollywood, ca. 1913

A. G. Schloesser, built his fantasy mansion Glengarry Castle in the foothills at Franklin and Argyle in 1909. A mad collection of various castle-like elements, it was described as a "pretentious mansion" with artistic decorations of the Louis XV and Flemish periods created by Italian and German artists of note. Later it was joined by his Sans Souci Castle across the street, which was another bizarre house with

overtones of baronial English and German Rhine castles. It doubled as the Kaiser's house when filmmaker Mack Sennett featured the exterior in an antiwar propaganda film.

On the crest of a nearby hill, an equally out-of-place Japanese palace was built in 1914 by millionaire silk trader Adolph Bernheimer and his brother Eugene. The residence and surrounding gardens, which cascaded down the hillside, were visible from most points in Hollywood. A showplace of imported Oriental antiques, dense, garish interiors, and gardens sprinkled with fountains and pagodas, it drew visitors from around the world, thereby advancing the image of Southern California as a unique and unusual place.

California's position as a magnet for nonconformist beliefs further enhanced the construction of buildings in Hollywood. Several structures were built in conjunction with new philosophies and religions brought to the area. Krotona, a branch of the Adyar Theosophists, set up shop in 1912 in Hollywood and created a mosque-like temple complex and grounds in the foothills above the commercial district. Later, branches of the Self-Realization Fellowship would appear on Sunset Boulevard as well as farther down the coast in Encinitas, with both locations having buildings of Middle Eastern design. Outside of Southern California, numerous buildings of a similar style appeared up and down the coast. Among them, the Rosicrucian Order established its headquarters in San Jose in 1927. Reflecting its metaphysical and mystic background, the compound featured Egyptian-influenced buildings and grounds.

Predating the Rosicrucians' endeavors was an "Egyptomania" phenomenon that occurred in the early 1920s. Particularly infectious in Southern California, where a comparable Mediterranean climate no doubt encouraged entrepreneurs to adopt it, the Egyptian Revival was brought on in part by the discovery of King Tutankhamun's tomb in 1922. An

STAR FLOWER SHOP
ARTISTIC DESIGNING
FREE DELIVERY
Van de Kamps Holland-Dutch BAKERY
Van de Kamps Holland-Dutch BAKERY
Van de Kamp's
Van de Kamps Holland-Dutch BAKERY
4115
OWER SHOP 4117 "SAY IT WITH FLOWERS"
Van de Kamps BAKERY
PIES
Bronson Meat
Quality
Service

OPPOSITE
Van de Kamp's Bakery, Los Angeles, ca. 1928. Architect: Harry Oliver

RIGHT
Tam o' Shanter Inn, 2980 Los Feliz Boulevard, Los Angeles, ca. 1922. Architect: Harry Oliver

impromptu and short-lived Egyptian-inspired building boom reinforced the concept of anything goes in California. For several years, hotels, apartments, movie theaters, car repair garages, real estate offices, plunges, and cafés received the Egyptian touch.

The heyday of California's programmatic past coincided with two developments, one local, one national. The rise of filmmaking in Hollywood and the widespread acceptance of the affordable automobile would combine to make California, and particularly Southern California, a hotbed of unusual architecture in the 1920s and 1930s.

Hollywood's influence on California's mimetic architecture was very direct. The tone of fantasy was encouraged once the studios congregated in and around Hollywood, with the architecture and sets associated with movie making affecting the local environment. While most early studio architecture remained nondescript, several studios did create facades that matched the fantasy of the filming behind their gates. Around 1910, the Selig Studio in Edendale, a few miles northeast of downtown Los Angeles, was constructed to look like nearby San Gabriel Mission, complete with tower and bells. By 1921, Charlie Chaplin and his brother Syd had completed their studio at Sunset and La Brea in a series of buildings in the English Tudor Style. Out in Culver City, Thomas Ince built his Ince Studio Building (1919) in a graceful adaptation of a Southern mansion.

Several blocks away, studio head Irvin Willat went one step further in bringing Hollywood onto the streets when he employed set designer Harry Oliver to construct a studio headquarters for him in 1921 on highly traveled Washington Boulevard. In a head-spinning evocation of a fairy-tale witch's house straight out of "Hansel and Gretel," Oliver transferred his cinematic set skills to the public sector. With this building, the connection between fantasy and reality was firmly made. The studio building remained as a local landmark until 1929, when it was

purchased by producer Ward Lascelle and moved to Beverly Hills, where it became his residence.

After designing the Willat Studio, Harry Oliver, who was also an art director for Fox and Metro studios, continued to use his movie background in various building projects outside the studio confines. Using a collection of postcards for inspiration, he created English thatched-roof apartments and Egyptian-inspired flats. Having caught the public's eye, he was soon asked to design the Van de Kamp's Bakery retail outlets for Lawrence Frank and Theodore Van de Kamp in 1921. At his clients' request, Oliver built the bakery outlets in the shape of small-scale Dutch windmills. As with the Willat Studio, the architect dramatized their appearance to make them more eye-catching. They were also to be portable so that in the event a location wasn't profitable they could be easily loaded on a truck and moved. Placed throughout Southern California, the dozens of fanciful structures again made a direct connection from studio lot to the urban roadside that further fueled California's car-crazy reputation.

Pleased with their bakery design, the Van de Kamp family employed Oliver for another venture on the "outskirts" of Los Angeles near Glendale. Montgomery's Country Inn, which would later be named the Tam o' Shanter, opened in 1922 on Tropico Avenue, later renamed Los Feliz Boulevard. Again following the family's wishes, Oliver designed a structure that would attract the interest of people driving by: "Make it fanciful. Make it a real standout. I want it to look like something out of Normandy" was owner Lawrence Frank's request. Oliver complied by creating another structure that looked like a transplanted movie set. Using a visual language similar to the one he used for the Willat Studio, Oliver created the roadside stop as a rambling fairy-tale structure complete with wavy rooflines, lopsided windows, and handmade lanterns partially trimmed in neon. The interior featured aged walls and soft curves that resembled the cottage of

OPPOSITE
*Robin Hood* set, Formosa Avenue and Santa Monica Boulevard, Los Angeles, ca. 1921

RIGHT
Grauman's Egyptian Theatre, 6712 Hollywood Boulevard, ca. 1922

Snow White. The restaurant also initiated car service, thereby making it the first in California to do so.

Compounding the fantasy aspect of Los Angeles and reinforcing the Hollywood connection, the buildings gave visitors and Angelenos glimpses of the illusion being created behind the studio walls as they drove around the city. The set for D. W. Griffith's *Intolerance* was built in 1916 at the corner of Sunset and Hollywood Boulevards. It displayed trussed and false-fronted Babylonia that was viewed by local residents and tourists years after the movie was filmed. Near the intersection of Santa Monica Boulevard and La Brea Avenue, the massive castle for Douglas Fairbanks's 1922 film *Robin Hood* towered surrealistically over the neighborhood. Several years later at the same location, the city of Baghdad would be created for another Fairbanks swashbuckler in an even larger set that was visible for blocks surrounding the studio. Throughout the area, false skies painted on billboard-size backdrops could be seen along the streets, while wooden dinosaur skeletons bordered studio fences. "Hollywood" appeared to be everywhere.

The influence of the movie studios on local architecture was noted early on by the media in several articles dating from the late 1920s. A 1928 article in the *Ice Cream Trade Journal* wrote in response to the highly profitable roadside stands:

> *"If this manufacturer had traveled through California without pre-warning and without stopping to investigate, he might have come away with the idea that the movie people had been so rash as to invade even the residential districts of the cities there in establishing locations. What else could a tourist think who, knowing by hearsay something of the prevalence of studios and the studio folk in that state, found himself whirling past gigantic ice cream freezers, snow block Eskimo igloos glowing in an electric aurora borealis by night, mammoth*

LEFT
Los Feliz Hills Real Estate Office, Los Angeles, ca. 1927

OPPOSITE
Wigwam Orange Stand, Foothill Boulevard, Arcadia, ca. 1927

*ice cream cones, and sparkling ice caverns, all established on the city streets or at vantage points along the open highway?"*

The contribution of art director to the architectural landscape of Los Angeles was noted in the January 1926 issue of *The Motion Picture Director* magazine:

*"In California, I believe, before elsewhere in America, a direct influence of the cinema upon the House that Jack Builds becomes evident. Here may be traced even the story types. A popular story is made having as locale a mythical village in middle Europe. And appear as if by magic, in the way of the West, castles and cottages patterned after castles and cottages of that village, existing only yesterday as a vision of the art director, today in wallboard and plaster on the studio lot, and tomorrow as ashes in an incinerator, where the studio refuse is destroyed. Stories of ancient Egypt appear — an entire block becomes reminiscent of Karnac and Luxor, sheltering countless dreamy-eyed and full-lipped Cleopatras from as far away as Far Rockaway even, who may lead you to a vacant seat. China and Russia have been seen in a photoplay. Then again on a street in Our Town."*

When it opened on October 18, 1922, the Egyptian Theatre on Hollywood Boulevard was a movie palace on a par with the ancient tomb of Tutankhamun, which would be discovered a month later. Lured to Hollywood by real estate developer Charles Toberman, Sid Grauman brought a touch of the Nile to the middle of filmland. A magnificent blending of kitsch and class, the structure was designed by the firm of Meyer and Holler. The forecourt featured palm trees, hieroglyphics, and stores masquerading as a bazaar. Above the main entrance an actor costumed as an Egyptian guard roamed the parapet announcing the start of each performance. Attendants

attired in period outfits led patrons to their seats. Here Sid Grauman initiated and refined the movie premiere by drawing movie stars and the attention of the world to his Hollywood theater. It was another grand illusion on the city streets.

While this concentration of movie-town architecture became synonymous with Hollywood, the rest of Southern California was beginning to blossom with startling architecture. By the mid-1920s, California's unusual architectural development had begun in earnest. A bright economy, rampant speculation and inexpensive real estate, endless boosterism, the geographic layout of the region, and the acceptance and fostering of the car culture all combined to make an environment conducive to this building type.

Proliferating in a short span of time, entrepreneurship, imagination, and the ingenuity of the small businessperson all contributed heavily to the success of many of these retail buildings. Promoted by the media as typical Southern California, the buildings supposedly lined the streets, but this notion was somewhat off base. The wide distances separating various suburban communities contradicted that image. The buildings were more like exclamation points along the highway. Still, there were far more of these structures in the Los Angeles area than was generally thought, and when added together they set California apart from any other region.

*Fortune* magazine, in a story about the lucrative American roadside, reinforced this idea of "the land of the bizarre" in a caption accompanying the photo of a stand featuring an oversized ice cream carton:

> *"The eye is quicker than the brain and therefore Freda Farms near Hartford, Connecticut, does very nicely. So do stands built like tamales, tea rooms built like teapots, papier-mache owls lettered 'I Scream,' laughing swine with neon teeth (again a tamale stand), and in fact almost any eye-widening*

LEFT
The Freezer, 3641 Pico Boulevard, Los Angeles, ca. 1932

OPPOSITE
Sherman Oaks service station, 15362 Ventura Boulevard, ca. 1933

*outlandishness you can imagine. To behold such haywire crown and seated in its ultimate glory, you must go to California."*

Throughout California, the main roads leading into metropolitan areas were the obvious place for refreshment stands, eateries, and other businesses to solicit the auto trade with unusual imagery. Enticing motorists who were driving by at 35 miles per hour required eye-catching and flashy solutions. While many commercial ventures warranted locations that would provide a financial return in relation to their investment, these simple roadside businesses could afford to be placed in less desirable and out-of-the-way urban and rural settings. The only mandate was that they be situated near or on a highly traveled street or thoroughfare.

In Duarte, on Foothill Boulevard, the Indian Village and Zanzibar Café (circa 1926) was typical of these roadside stops. The combination roadside stand and restaurant catered to the traveler and tourist heading into Los Angeles by selling produce and orange juice. Clearly not Native American in image, the Indian Village was exotic looking and enticed customers to stop in. Later named the Wigwam, it featured food and furniture made from local orange wood. Closer to town, but in an area still considered rural in the 1920s, the Zulu Hut (circa 1926) on Ventura Boulevard near Universal Studios was a café that attempted a similar exotic reference: Africa. Owner Raymond McKee dressed his servers in grass skirts and blackface for an "authentic" trip to the "Dark Continent." Several three-dimensional oranges and lemons could be found in the regions outside L.A. where "fresh squeezed orange juice" was available almost everywhere, especially at the Baldy Inn (1927), a stucco re-creation of the mountain range it faced.

Within L.A.'s urban spread, the evolving commercial strip of Washington Boulevard in Culver City was littered with a series of fantasy buildings. A precursor

BLU-GREEN
GAS
GAS & OIL ACCESSORIES
SHERMAN OAKS SERVICE STA.
15362
LADIES

to filmland's famed Sunset Strip, this main artery to the beach also served as a direct route to the many studios in Culver City. Washington Boulevard's popularity was enhanced during Prohibition by its reputation as a stretch of roadway on which one could score some illegal booze, gamble, and "raise a little Cain." This series of buildings, all with programmatic intonations, lined the street from the eastern border of Culver City westward. Among them were the following: the Mission Village (1929), the Monkey Farm (1925), the Fireplace (1927), Mammy's Shack (1930), King's Tropical Inn (1926), Lighthouse Gardens (1927), the Royal Barbecue (1924), Jerry's Cabin Café (1926), The Hoosegow (1927), the Ham Tree (1929), Jesse James Cabin (1928), the Green Mill (1919), the Irvin Willat Studio (1921), Thomas Ince Studio (1919), the Barrel Café (1934), Roscoe "Fatty" Arbuckle's Plantation Café (1928), and the Pup Café (circa 1930), among others. In describing the Royal Barbecue, a 1924 trade magazine gave uncanny insight to the place and time of this rural/urban roadside stop:

> *"The quaintness of a medieval inn, as idealized and enhanced by the spirit of jazz, is the atmosphere that has been achieved by the little Royal Barbecue Inn which has risen on Washington Boulevard between Los Angeles and the beach. The building was designed by its owner and manager, Mrs. Josephine Lanzit, in co-operation with her brother, E. J. Reutler, who was also the builder. It is one of those rambling crazily artistic structures, imitating a tumble-down medieval dwelling, but for all its playful imitation of age, not only modern but*

*distinctively futuristic in effect and charming, like a very young girl masquerading in her own idea of an ancient costume. There is probably no stretch of highway on the Pacific coast which is more constantly traveled by pleasuring auto parties than that between the beach and Los Angeles, and so those who serve the pleasure-seeking public have not been slow in congregating on it. A number of the largest and most brilliant road-house cafés like the Green Mill and Plantation are located there and also a large number of 'barbecued sandwich' shacks line the road."*

In time the urban strip became the most viable location for the ever-increasing number of oddball buildings. Some of the most popular imagery on the byways during this time was reserved for businesses selling ice cream products. Alluding to colder climes were ice cream stands such as the Igloo (1928), complete with miniature polar bear and frozen ghost frigate bathed in the Northern Lights; the Ice Palace (1929); and the Ice Castle (1928). The Big Cone (1928) was a chain of ice cream stands in the shape of a 20-foot sugar cone made of metal and placed from Laguna Beach to the San Fernando Valley. The Big Freezer (1927) chain was owned by United Sweet Shops of Glendale, California. Numbering 20 by 1929, their appeal to the automobile was no mistake. The old-fashioned freezer, originally painted an authentic wood brown, was later repainted white with red hoops to be visible from a long distance. Company owners claimed the following as one of the many advantages of the Big Freezer:

SIGNAL
TRY THE NEW OIL THAT...
reduces engine wear 50%
MOTOR OIL
LEE TIRES

PAGE 56
Aztec Hotel, 311 West Foothill Boulevard, Monrovia, ca. 1925. Architect: Robert Stacy-Judd

PAGE 57
Angeles Abbey, 1515 East Compton Boulevard, Compton, ca. 1924

OPPOSITE
Signal service station, Los Angeles, 1951

RIGHT
Jack Johnson Co. Roofing & Painting, Oakland, ca. 1927

*"The building advertises its own product and is considered by authorities to be the most successful wayside store so far invented. The traveler cannot mistake the purpose of the freezer when he sees it ahead of him beside the highway. He knows that there is a place where ice cream is sold. The plan of having a building cry its own product is of distinct advantage in wayside places because if the automobile driver does not sense the fact that a certain store along the way sells ice cream until he is past it, then that possible customer is lost for he cannot, in the face of traffic, turn around and come back."*

To further attract roadside attention, Big Freezer owners installed a revolving handle that they claimed increased sales by 50 percent the first week it was available. The simple building made of steel had no plumbing, tables, or toilets (employees were encouraged to use neighboring businesses for their needs), but just a simple counter where prepackaged bulk ice cream was sold because "the ice cream for the most part is eaten in automobiles." This pared-down layout allowed for the buildings to be moved at will if the location proved unsatisfactory or if the lot was slated for a permanent building. Perfectly dovetailing with California's expanding urban car culture, the Big Freezers were not located in the open country as many other wayside stands were, but placed "in cities on vacant lots in sections where traffic is considerable but always where there is ample parking space for a car to stop in front."

As the Southern California geography began to fill in through rapid development, many of these wayside places found themselves in transitional locations between open country and suburban towns. Characteristic of this change was the Aztec Hotel (1925). Located on Foothill Boulevard, which was a major highway leading into Los Angeles, the Aztec Hotel was built in the suburban community, of Monrovia. Designed by architect Robert

Stacy-Judd from his offices in Hollywood, it was described in a trade magazine of the period as being "designed after Aztec and Mayan styles with furnishings and fixtures carried out in weird and fascinating details which leave little to the imagination." Stacy-Judd focused a major part of his career on re-creating the architecture of ancient North American cultures. Before this commission he had toyed with various other exotic period-revival buildings including a proposal for an Egyptian-inspired theater in nearby Arcadia. Although his later influences were distinctly Mayan, he felt Mayan architecture wasn't as widely known. The hotel was named "The Aztec" because he speculated it was a name more familiar to the general public. Stacy-Judd meticulously researched many of the details for the hotel before modifying and adapting them to a modern California setting. Included in the hotel design were stylized Mayan interiors for the lobby that expressed the feel of entering a temple

dwelling. In an odd juxtaposition, an adjoining coffee shop and soda fountain also received the Mayan treatment.

Further exercising his creative muscle, Stacy-Judd was engaged to create an Indian village–style resort at Soboba Hot Springs some 90 miles east of Los Angeles near San Jacinto. Between 1924 and 1927, a series of cottages were interspersed on the hillside representing various Native American settlements. Taking stylistic liberties, his freestanding rooms were playful interpretations of Pueblo, Hopi, Yuma, and other Southwest tribal dwellings. A proposed hotel and bathhouse in similar styles never materialized, but the dozen cottages built were extremely popular with visitors at the time. Another resort closer to Los Angeles in the Chatsworth area was also to be a cluster of Mayan and Indian structures in a development called Twin Lakes Park. Advertised in 1927 as the "Homesite of the Maya Village," the resort had an entry gate in a vaguely Mayan style, but again,

PREVIOUS SPREAD
Umbrella service station, 830 South La Brea Avenue, Los Angeles, ca. 1931
LEFT
California Flower Show, Los Angeles, 1921
OPPOSITE
Big Donut Drive-In, 805 West Manchester Boulevard, Inglewood, ca. 1955

a proposed clubhouse and cabins never materialized.

Robert Stacy-Judd created several other buildings and residences in modified Mayan and Pueblo styles. Cliff-dwelling-style apartments in Elysian Park, a church in Ventura, a Masonic temple, and several homes in North Hollywood were built in the twenties and thirties. Still, most of his more ostentatious commissions were never realized.

The idea of Los Angeles as an exotic destination was long promoted by the region's real estate agents and promoters and supported in many of the buildings that were built there in the 1920s. Many of the buildings transcended the mere convention of reviving historical styles. For example, the proximity of California's desert inspired a wide selection of Moorish and Mediterranean buildings that were spread throughout Southern California. Angeles Abbey, a cemetery complex in Compton, flaunted palm trees, tiled domes, and Moroccan-style arches. In the Mar Vista district, a drive-in open-air market of Middle Eastern design was built with a dome-topped tower and a colonnade of Oriental arches. The real estate offices for the Girard subdivision (1928) at Topanga Canyon and Ventura Boulevards were fashioned in a similar mosque-and-minaret motif, but their interiors were vacant, thus the buildings served as props. In 1927, Calpet Petroleum built an extravagant station catering to wealthy Angelenos on Wilshire Boulevard. Located in what was then one of L.A.'s most fashionable shopping districts, the station had a vaguely Middle Eastern tone. A Tunisian color scheme of red, tan, and black was used for the tile work. Catering to its 55 percent female customers were a "colored liveried footman" and a team of eight service men outfitted in maroon jackets, white shirts, black bow ties, breeches, and puttees. The ladies' room was decorated with Venetian mirrors and a "red leather topped wicker settee with lovely pillows, a number of rockers, a taupe rug, and smoking stands."

BIG DONUT DRIVE-IN
COCKTAILS
CHUCKWAG
ALL YOU CAN EAT
OPEN 7 DAYS
CARS PLEASE FOLLOW ARROW
DO-NUTS
PLEASE USE
RUBBISH CONTAINERS

The main room was enclosed by wrought iron gates and a white cash register rested on a marble-topped table beneath a chandelier. Samson's Tire Works (1929), on the outskirts of Los Angeles, paid tribute to the connection of oil and the Middle East with its magnificent re-creation of an Assyrian palace. Designed by the firm of Morgan, Walls, and Clements, the main building and wall fronted the street while behind the decorative walls a modern factory churned out tires with no pretensions to fantasy.

Grauman's Chinese Theatre (1927) contributed a grand pastiche of Asian elements suggesting a mysterious and exotic location. Perfectly matching the illusion of moviemaking, the theater borrowed pieces of Chinese architecture and put them together facing the main street of the movies, Hollywood Boulevard. Acknowledging the importance of the automobile, an open forecourt gestured directly to the street and became the central plaza for the theater's famed premieres. An extravagant interior was lavishly appointed with murals, chandeliers, and intricate details such as the costumes of the ushers and the faucets in the washrooms. Along the same Asian lines, the Mandarin Market (circa 1929), a drive-in arcade on Vine Street, was the commercial equivalent to the high-toned Chinese Theatre. An incongruous Chilitown Café, which anchored one of the retail outlets, spoke much about the seriousness of the imagery of architectural anomalies.

In extending the search for more exotic solutions, Native American imagery was tapped not only for its references to the Old West but also for the intrigue of relatively obscure ancient American civilizations. Satisfying this criterion was the Mayan Theatre (1927) in downtown Los Angeles, the Cliff Dwellers Café (1927) on Beverly Boulevard, the TeePee drive-in restaurant (1931) in the Belmont Shores district of Long Beach, the Hotel Tahquitz (1929) in Palm Springs, the pueblo-inspired Alessandro Hotel in Hemet (1928), the

OPPOSITE
Herbert's Drive-In, Fairfax Avenue and Beverly Boulevard, Los Angeles, ca. 1939

BELOW
Barkies/The Pup, 3649 Beverly Boulevard, Los Angeles, ca. 1936

Tower Auto Court (1929) on Ventura Boulevard, and the Mission Village (1932) near Culver City, which offered a range of Native American styles in a motel, trailer court, and tourist complex.

The golden age of this architectural type lasted for approximately 10 years, from 1924 through 1934. Within that span the best buildings in this architectural category were built: the Hoot Hoot I Scream stand (1930), the Pup and Bulldog Cafés (circa 1930 and 1927, respectively), the Sphinx Realty building (1926), the Mushrooms restaurant (circa 1928), the Zep Diner (1930), the Hollywood Flower Pot (circa 1930), the Cream Can (circa 1928), the Tamale (1928), the Toed Inn (1931), the Pumpkin Palace (1927), the Mother Goose Pantry (1929), the Big Red Piano (1930), and many others. And most had stories to tell.

The Brown Derby (1926) symbolized the apex of this building spree. One of the most popular examples of this architectural genre, it owed much of its fame to its celebrity pedigree. The owners included film producer and taste arbiter Herbert Somborn, once married to Gloria Swanson; Broadway wit Wilson Mizner, who is credited with naming it; Charles "Buddy" Rogers; Jack Warner; and the department store scions Tom and Wilbur May. All were interested in investing in a place that stayed open late and offered good, substantial food. Somborn reasoned that "a place that served fine American dishes made with the freshest and best raw materials obtainable, prepared with skill and experience, a place so distinctive in architecture that, once seen or heard about, it would never again be forgotten." Opening night guests included Mary Pickford, Sid Grauman, Loretta Young, Bebe Daniels, and Corinne Griffith. Far from being a gourmand's paradise, the Brown Derby initially offered hot dogs, hamburgers, grilled cheese sandwiches, chili, tamales, coffee, tea, milk, and near beer — in other words, diner fare. Being across the street from the famed Ambassador Hotel and Cocoanut Grove secured a steady clientele of stars that in turn brought the fans, which made the Derby an instant, and ongoing hit.

Joining the evolving carscape was a host of advertising sculptures posted along the streets that added another dimension to the byways. Reviled by critics as another element of blight to an overcrowded streetscape, these three-dimensional figures on pedestals were used to sell just about any product a local resident might consume or any place a local resident might visit. Using the same eye-catching principle as shaped buildings, the sculptures were meant to grab your attention for a billboard moment and fade away just as quickly. The Richfield gas station featured a model of driver Barney Oldfield and his race car. A Colonial-style dame surmounted the Carthay Circle Theatre pedestal (1927); bathing beauties frolicked

OPPOSITE
Beany's, Pacific Coast Highway at Ximeno Avenue, Long Beach, ca. 1955
RIGHT
Currie's Ice Cream, Los Angeles, ca. 1953

on the Sea Breeze Beach Club sign, and Ye Bull Pen Inn had a majestic bull atop its platform. Another curious element to the streetscape was the miniature golf courses, which sprouted up almost overnight in a craze that started in 1930. Bringing a whole new level of zaniness to the Los Angeles area, this transitory fad took advantage of a relatively low investment and the large supply of vacant lots. Hundreds of these courses were found throughout the city, and miniature cabins, rock grottoes, windmills, and rustic bridges were added to city corners everywhere. One ambitious course took the theme of the frozen North and constructed an oversized igloo, abandoned ghost ships, and snowbound paths. Movie star Mary Pickford invested in one grandiose course at the corner of Wilshire and La Cienega Boulevards in Beverly Hills in 1930. The Wilshire Links course featured a Zigzag Moderne advertising pylon that housed a corner office and refreshment stand. Scattered throughout the layout were stylized palm trees that looked like props from a German Expressionist film.

The Depression, during which many of these structures were built, rarely deterred the construction of these type of buildings. The inexpensive nature of a modest building and the still-affordable land made many of these investments worthwhile.

Some of these ventures proved so successful that the owners went on to construct multiple units and even chains. The Twin Barrels drive-in (1928) and the Bucket (circa 1935) were among those that built several units. The Sanders System drive-in restaurant, in the shape of giant coffee pots spouting steam, staked out major intersections and opened three units in July 1930. In Tinseltown tradition, klieg lights crossed the skies, bands were broadcast live, and celebrities were on hand to cut the ribbon. The Chili Bowl restaurants, with 23 units, outperformed most of its competitors. Started in 1931 by entrepreneur Arthur Whizin, their enormous success was due to the simple fare, affordable

GET THE
CHILI BOWL
GRILL-BURGERS
EGGROYAL
SIZE
HABIT!
3012 Crenshaw Boulevard
Near Jefferson Blvd.
Los Angeles
2228 E. Florence Avenue
Near Santa Fe Ave.
Huntington Park
801 N. La Brea
Near Melrose Ave.
Hollywood
"SIZE"

OPPOSITE
Chili Bowl menu, ca. 1933
RIGHT
White Log Tavern, Los Angeles, ca. 1934

prices, and Whizin's tireless promotion. Found mostly in urban areas, the White Log Taverns, which originated in Oakland, spread 40 units across California and into Oregon with the same "immaculate early American colonial style" log cabin. Out in the open, along California roads, the Jumbo Lemon Company produced its one-man booths from Yuma to Yreka along most of the main highways in California, and in small towns. The owners avoided large cities such as Los Angeles and San Francisco. The Giant Orange refreshment stands ran the length of the San Joaquin Valley on Highways 40, 50, and 99 with a total of 16 stands at their peak.

The concentration of programmatic structures in Southern California sometimes overshadowed the fact that these types of structures were actually dispersed throughout the state. In addition to lemons and oranges, there were others. In San Jose the beacon from a 40-foot lighthouse that rose above the Grace Baptist Church could be seen for 20 miles in the Santa Clara Valley, so it was claimed. Merced had the Magnus Root Beer drive-in (circa 1934), an oversized root beer barrel. The first bona fide motel, the Motel Inn (1925), in San Luis Obispo, suggested an old mission with a replica of Santa Barbara's mission bell tower along Highway 101. In Carmel, the Tuck Box (1926), a tea shop, as well as other fairy-tale-like buildings were built by local resident Hugh Comstock. The Bay Area supplied numerous novelty buildings on the highways leading into San Francisco. Windmill-shaped hotels and stands could be found in the East Bay and along El Camino Real and Bayshore Highway where restaurants such as Dinah's (circa 1925) addressed the road. The high density of San Francisco made it a difficult location to transpose the roadside sensibilities of programmatic architecture. Instead, period revival examples stood in for most mimetic architecture with theaters such as the Alhambra (1926) on Polk Street and the Alexandria (circa 1923) on Geary. In Berkeley, several commercial buildings and apartments including the

LEFT
Twin Inns, Carlsbad, ca. 1932

OPPOSITE
Tail o' the Pup opening, 311 North La Cienega Boulevard, Los Angeles, 1946

Tupper and Reed Building (1925) appropriated the fantasy style of the late '20s and early '30s.

By the mid-1930s the building boom of architectural anomalies showed signs of exhaustion. While still lauded in the press, this informal movement fell out of favor as new architectural styles began to appear. Los Angeles, always receptive to change, embraced the new Streamline Moderne style, which was promoted by industrial designers and showcased in several national expositions. Almost instantly it became the style of choice for anything that was new, modern, and progressive. With the advent of clean lines and allusions to speed and the future, the construction of these oddball buildings began to dwindle. Only a few structures with programmatic leanings were able to accommodate the style. Robert Derrah designed the Coca-Cola Company Building in 1936 in the industrial section of L.A. to look like a streamlined ocean liner. He also produced the Crossroads of the World (1936) in Hollywood, an informal mall of assorted shops in various historical and period styles fitted around a stylized streamlined ship. Facing Sunset Boulevard at the end of the liner was a large pylon with a rotating globe trimmed in neon that beckoned autoists like a lighthouse. In San Francisco, the elegant Maritime Museum (1939) also referenced the Streamline Moderne style but in a way that suppressed any unusual subtext. Back in L.A., the Streamline Diner (1935) on San Vincente Boulevard successfully adopted the new styling in a tasteful restaurant, but it was the modern drive-in restaurant that supplanted the old rules of the road. Here, gleaming buildings, especially those designed by Harry Werner and Wayne McAllister, grabbed customers off the street with their tall neon-lit pylons. Expressing everything that was modern, the drive-in restaurant became a preferred roadside model in the late 1930s.

The early 1940s were lean years for any type of building as the specter of war

effectively tightened construction. Once the war began, rationed materials and travel limitations squelched an already moribund programmatic tradition. The war effort in Southern California did produce new methods and materials that would be used in the signage and statues, which in turn would become substitutes for many of the fast-disappearing structures of the '20s. It was in this critical period of disfavor that some of the best-shaped buildings disappeared. Never intended for long-term use, the buildings' fragile nature made them vulnerable to adverse conditions, and a crowded wartime L.A. made demands on every parcel of premium land.

With Modernist principles fully embraced at the end of World War II, not much interest was concentrated on building new programmatic structures. Despite this postwar slump, L.A. saw several structures pop up: The Tail o' the Pup, opened by two ex-GIs in 1946, was featured in a *LIFE* magazine spread that showed premiere-type crowds clamoring for hot dogs. Drivers encountered a surrealistic vision on Olympic Boulevard, where a retail outlet dispensed stockings beneath a giant 30-foot leg. The Sanderson Hosiery Company (1948), seizing on the advertising potential, inaugurated its company by hoisting movie celebrity Marie Wilson on a crane and releasing a giant garter from the gam. Up north, the Capitol Inn (1948) in Sacramento was built as a replica of what else—the state capitol.

Modernism crept into this building type in the slightest ways. Signs were the primary adjunct to pared-down retail outlets. In Currie's Ice Cream store (circa 1950), the giant cone formerly showcased atop the building was now discreetly placed near the sleek structure. As the old Van de Kamp's windmills disappeared from the street, modernizing included incorporating retail outlets into supermarkets or in some cases repackaging stores in modern buildings with only a neon sign as a reminder of the three-dimensional building. Based on popular cartoon characters, the Beanie and Cecil drive-in restaurant (circa 1952)

LEFT
Currie's advertisement, ca. 1949
OPPOSITE
Barkies, 3649 Beverly Boulevard, Los Angeles, ca. 1930

was housed in a pared-down box with a three-dimensional figure of Beanie as its sole attention-grabbing reference.

Most of the striking commercial statements of this era were reserved for signage, three-dimensional figures, and buildings that were simple to construct. This broadened idea of the programmatic shifted the emphasis of California's wacky reputation away from the old "dog and frog" standbys to these other areas. *Holiday* magazine noted this shift in a 1947 article entitled "California's Sunstruck Signs": "The bizarre competes with the screwloose in getting attention along the West Coast highways." Pictured was the Hangman's Tree (circa 1946), a San Fernando Valley eatery that advertised "warm beer and lousy food." Accompanying the sign was a mannequin hanging from a gallows.

The big figures and giant sculptures of men that were introduced in the '50s came courtesy of postwar technology. Their molded forms and generic interchangeable parts made them versatile advertising devices, and their low cost spread them statewide. In the Bay Area, the Doggie Diner (1948) snack shops had a variation on this theme in the giant cartoon dog's heads with chef hats that were hoisted on poles in front of each stand.

With an urban landscape rapidly closing in, the competition for customers' attention became acute and the luxury of open space and high visibility the first generation of buildings experienced was no longer there. The giant sign fulfilled the new roadside expectations. Russ Wendell realized this when he planned his Big Donut chain in 1949. By 1950 his dream was realized in the 30-foot donut he erected at the corner of Century Boulevard and Normandie Avenue. In true Southern California fashion, he debuted his donut in December with the fanfare of a Hollywood premiere. Clowns, jugglers, and magicians performed, free coffee and donuts were handed out, and a trapeze artist swung from the middle of the donut hole. At Christmastime, Santa and his reindeer were installed flying

TOASTED
BARKIES
No 4
No 4
SANDWICH SHOPS

through the same hole. The store was an instant hit and Wendell went on to build 10 more by 1956.

The California-born Googie Style, with its aggressive honesty, expressed materials, and sign presence, was a perfect segue from the more obvious revivalist architecture to a 1950s vocabulary. Expressing a "Jet Age" mentality, this new style was suggestive of a programmatic ideal but avoided any figurative referencing. The hamburger stands and coffee shops that effectively used Googie imagery maintained the advertising qualities of a building as a sign but rarely committed to a three-dimensional object as a sign.

The tide of criticism directed at roadside buildings began to turn by the early '60s as popular tastes evolved. In an article entitled "Who Killed Our Monstrosities?" one author commented, "All the buildings look the same. Glass upon glass, tile upon tile, floor upon floor. Nothing distinctive, like that giant-shaped dog on Washington Boulevard that once was—of course—a hot dog house. Los Angeles could use a little more honesty like that." With the lapse of time, a clearer picture of the historical significance of these structures emerged and critics began to reassess the sensibilities of roadside architecture. Movements such as "Pop Art" were also sympathetic to this architecture and were catalysts for removing the stigma associated with the nonconformist buildings in the '20s and '30s. But it was too late to save many of the structures as they crumbled or were dismantled to make way for new development.

While a few examples of the programmatic were built in the 1960s and '70s, the shape of new buildings was confined to simpler forms. New building restrictions and sign ordinances precluded the more organic shapes of the past that wood and stucco allowed. Instead, the embellished box became a transitional form. The Showboat (1968), a restaurant chain, created the illusion of a Mississippi paddle wheeler by hanging the decorative boat elements on a basic box. Likewise, the

OPPOSITE
Rosicrucian Park postcard, ca. 1940

RIGHT
Castle San Souci, Franklin Avenue at Argyle Avenue, Hollywood, 1908. Owner: Dr. Alfred Schloesser

Fleetwood Building (1987) on Ventura Boulevard in Woodland Hills fashioned a facade of Cadillac parts and painted the whole structure bright pink to draw more attention to the simple form. In Turlock, the United Equipment Company erected a building that looked like a two-story tractor for its offices (1977). Again, to a simple box was added the apparatus of a bulldozer complete with a scraper pushing rocks. Visible from Highway 99, the building was based on one the owner had seen on a visit to Japan. The Shutter Shack (1977) in Westminster, California, exhibited the possibilities of a one-person box. Sheathed with some simple additions such as a lens and flash cube, the Shutter Shack was made to look like a 35-millimeter camera. While not the most satisfying of buildings, these structures did keep this style alive.

Just before the roadside tradition was entirely depleted in the 1980s, a renewal of the vernacular spirit ensued. Fueled in part by preservation efforts and the wealth of information unearthed in reexamining the legacy of the roadside, new buildings were taking the place of those that were destroyed. The more successful examples bypassed a cloying nostalgia for a contemporary version of the programmatic past. The Hamburger That Ate L.A. (1989) was a three-dimensional facade of a hamburger accompanied by a stylized version of L.A. City Hall that had a bite extracted from it.

In the '90s, a certain legitimacy descended on architectural aberrations when established architects began to adopt a formalized version of roadside architecture. The Disney Company stepped up to the plate when it hired well-known architect Michael Graves to design a new Team Disney headquarters on its Burbank lot. A postmodern tour de force, the building features a pediment held up by massive statues of the "Seven Dwarfs." Across the street, a new animation building that is highly visible from an adjacent freeway is rimmed by a stylized filmstrip and capped with the alchemist's hat worn by Mickey Mouse in the "Sorcerer's Apprentice" sequence from

LEFT
The Darkroom advertisement, 1939

OPPOSITE
Sanderson Hosiery, 11711 Olympic Boulevard, West Los Angeles, 1949. Owner: A. A. Sanderson

the Disney film *Fantasia*. The hat is several stories high. Universal Studios also contributed to this themed architecture in its CityWalk (1993) expansion by Jon Jerde. A giant jukebox and an oversized surfboard were part of the fabricated, urban, street mall decorated with neon and other street elements. In Venice, California, the Chiat/Day advertising agency commissioned Frank Gehry to design its building (1991), which includes a giant pair of binoculars by Claes Oldenburg and Coosje van Bruggen. An immediate landmark, and later to become Google's Southern California outpost, the binoculars serve as the portal to an underground parking structure. The stem of the binoculars contains several conference rooms lit by skylights in the lenses.

Meanwhile, the highly visible projects produced in Las Vegas did not deter others from producing their own personal versions of unusual buildings. Although not as ambitious as the deep-pocket ventures of large companies, these new eye-popping projects remain true to the basic premise of advertising: amuse viewers and attract attention. The various molded figures that have been so popular in the upper Midwest, the latest giant inflatables, and the ongoing, personal, three-dimensional statements of these new projects promise a healthy future for the programmatic in California, throughout the United States, and around the world.

The future development of roadside vernacular architecture is open for all sorts of meanderings and interpretations. If the checkered history of mimetic architecture — from advertising elephants to modest roadside stands to corporate buildings — is any indication of the future, the evolution of this intriguing style of architecture will be fascinating to follow. The accelerated international presence of such buildings seems to indicate that the world is now the stage for the California Crazy phenomenon.

NYL

STOP & SIP
BEN-HUR
DRIP
EAT IN CAR

BEN-HUR
COFFEE
WILSHIRE
COFFEE POT

HEALTH TRIUMPHANT
Horton & Converse
PRESCRIPTION PHARMACISTS
LOS ANGELES
HOLLYWOOD
BEVERLY HILLS

PREVIOUS SPREAD
Coffee Pot, 8601 Wilshire Boulevard, Los Angeles, ca. 1935

OPPOSITE
Horton & Converse statue, Los Angeles, ca. 1927

ABOVE LEFT
Ute Chief Bottling Company statue, ca. 1929

ABOVE RIGHT
Sea Breeze Beach Club statue, Santa Monica, ca. 1927

ABOVE
La Brea Dog and Cat Hospital, 931 North La Brea Avenue, Los Angeles, ca. 1927

OPPOSITE
Hotel Chelsea statue, Los Angeles, ca. 1926

HOTEL
CHELSEA
200 ROOMS
HOTEL
CHELSEA
BONNIE BRAE
NEAR SIXTH
LOS ANGELES

ABOVE

Richfield Oil Company statue, Los Angeles, ca. 1928

RIGHT

Richfield Oil Company advertisement, 1925

OPPOSITE

*Popular Mechanics* article, 1935

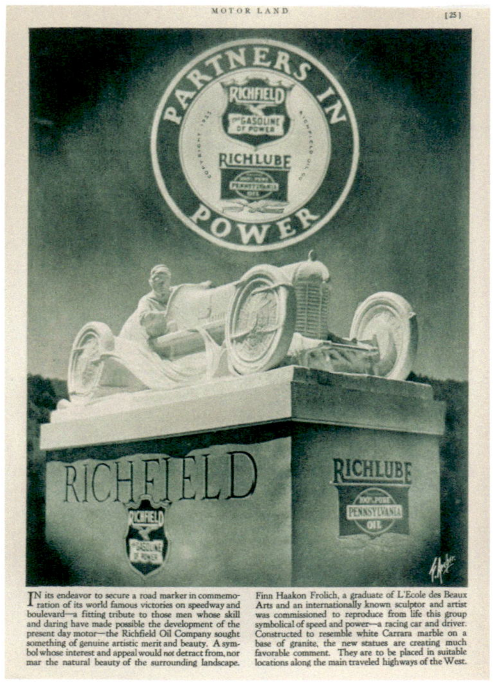


IN its endeavor to secure a road marker in commemoration of its world famous victories on speedway and boulevard—a fitting tribute to those men whose skill and daring have made possible the development of the present day motor—the Richfield Oil Company sought something of genuine artistic merit and beauty. A symbol whose interest and appeal would *not* detract from, nor mar the natural beauty of the surrounding landscape.

Finn Haakon Frolich, a graduate of L'Ecole des Beaux Arts and an internationally known sculptor and artist was commissioned to reproduce from life this group symbolical of speed and power—a racing car and driver. Constructed to resemble white Carrara marble on a base of granite, the new statues are creating much favorable comment. They are to be placed in suitable locations along the main traveled highways of the West.

# Plastic Statues Supplant Roadside Billboards

*Above, Dairy Farm Uses Statues of Mother and Child with Cow to Advertise Its Products along Highway*

*Plastic Sculpture Is Becoming Popular with Highway Advertisers in the West; Statues Dramatizing the Product Are Molded, Set on a Firm Base, Then Lacquered to Resist Weathering; Above, Statue of Knight on Horse Advertises Hollywood Pharmacist; Left, Plastic Bell Boy Attracts Motorists to Hotel*

*Statue of Bull, Above, Advertises "Ye Bull Pen Inn"; Long in Use, It Shows Effect of Weathering; Below, at Right, Model of Race Car Advertises Brand of Gasoline; Properly Lacquered, These Statues Withstand Weather for Considerable Periods and Are Seldom Attacked by Vandals; Although Billboards Sometimes Cause Protests against Disfiguring Landscape, the Motoring Public Does Not Seem to Object to Roadside Sculpture; Statues Are Cast from Molds and Are Relatively Inexpensive to Manufacture*

Wilshire
Cochran
APTS.
SINGLES-DOUBLES
BOBS AIRMAIL
METRO

FOR
RENT
DOUBLES
SINGLES
RVICE
FASTER – ITS BETTER
Willard
US
General
Mobilgas
US
General
Mobilgas

PREVIOUS SPREAD
Bob's Airmail Service, 5433 Wilshire Boulevard, Los Angeles, ca. 1935

LEFT
Airplane Café, Los Angeles, ca. 1924

BELOW
Airplane service station, Ventura Boulevard and Ventura Place, Studio City, ca. 1941

RIGHT
Airplane service station, Studio City, ca. 1935

BELOW
Bob's Airmail Service brochure, ca. 1934

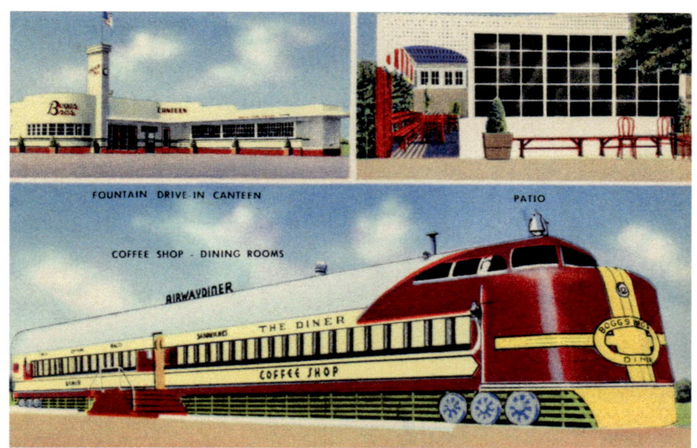


ABOVE
Friedhof's Airway Diner, 2521 Pacific Highway, San Diego, ca. 1946

LEFT
Boggs Bros. Airway Diner, 2521 Pacific Highway, San Diego, ca. 1947

OPPOSITE
Allied Model Trains, 4411 Sepulveda Boulevard, Culver City, 1989

ALLIED MODEL TRAINS
4411
CLOSED

LEFT
Toadstool, Panama-California Exposition, San Diego, 1917

BELOW
Scenic Railroad, Venice, ca. 1909

ABOVE

Amusement Zone, Venice, ca. 1909

RIGHT

Dragon Gorge, Venice, ca. 1910

GRAND CANYON
STEEL CARS
ENTRANCE
EXIT ONLY

OPPOSITE
Grand Canyon, Venice, ca. 1911
THIS PAGE
L. A. Thompson Scenic Railway, Venice, 1910

BELOW
Artichoke, 11261 Merritt Street, Castroville, 1984

OPPOSITE TOP
O'Neill House, 507 North Rodeo Drive, Beverly Hills, 1987

OPPOSITE BOTTOM
O'Neill House, 507 North Rodeo Drive, Beverly Hills, 2003

ASK MALONE
REALTOR
528
BAKER AVE.
THIS PROPERTY FOR SALE
ASK MALONE

Silk's
SUPREME
PREPARED
SPANISH
STYLE
RICE
-simply heat and eat
GET A CAN
FROM
Your Grocer
TODAY

OPPOSITE TOP
Ask Malone Realtor,
Los Angeles, ca. 1920

OPPOSITE BOTTOM
Silk's Spanish Rice,
Los Angeles, 1932

ABOVE
Pacific Homes, Los Angeles,
1926

RIGHT
Wynn's Tire & Rubber Co.
advertisement, ca. 1925

ABOVE
Mission Electric Co.,
San Francisco, ca. 1935

OPPOSITE TOP
D'Hot Dog, Los Angeles, 1979

OPPOSITE BOTTOM
Giant shoe, ca. 1939

D'HOT DOG
7512 SUNNY BRAE
CANOGA PARK, CA

PAPE

Aztec Hotel, 311 West Foothill Boulevard, Monrovia, ca. 1925. Architect: Robert Stacy-Judd

AZTEC HOTEL, MONROVIA, CALIF.

OPPOSITE TOP

Aztec Hotel postcard, ca. 1926

OPPOSITE BOTTOM

Aztec Hotel advertisement, 1929

THIS PAGE

Aztec Hotel, 311 West Foothill Boulevard, Monrovia, 1979. Architect: Robert Stacy-Judd

LEFT
Barkies matchcover, ca. 1939

BELOW
Barkies, 3649 Beverly Boulevard, Los Angeles, ca. 1928

OPPOSITE
Barkies, 3649 Beverly Boulevard, Los Angeles, ca. 1929

TOASTED
BARKIES
THE QUALITY FRANKFURTER
Barbecue Sandwiches Waffles
Toasted Sandwiches Waffles
SANDWICH SHOPS
B
OPEN
OPEN
3049
We Sell Christopher's ICE CREAM

ABOVE
Barrel Café, 5533 Huntington Drive, Los Angeles, ca. 1930

OPPOSITE TOP
Barrel Restaurant, Washington Boulevard, Culver City, ca. 1939

OPPOSITE BOTTOM
Barrel Club, Vallejo, ca. 1948

HAMBURGERS
CHILI
SPAGHETTI
MALTS

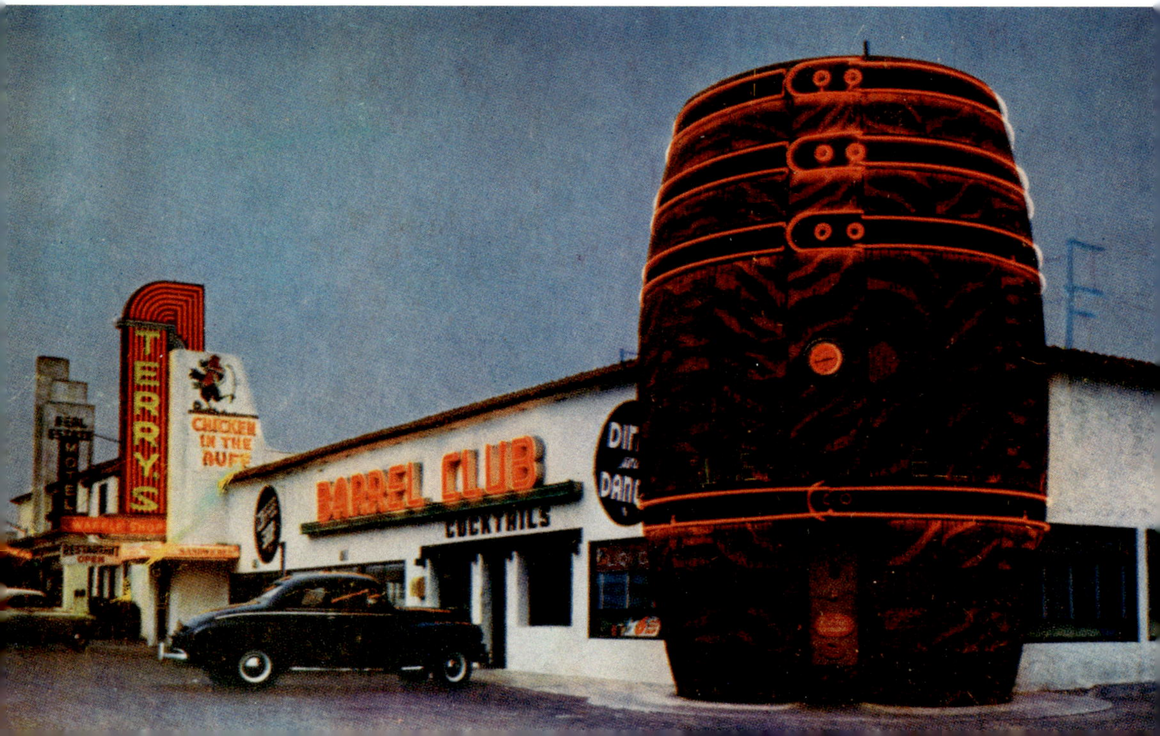

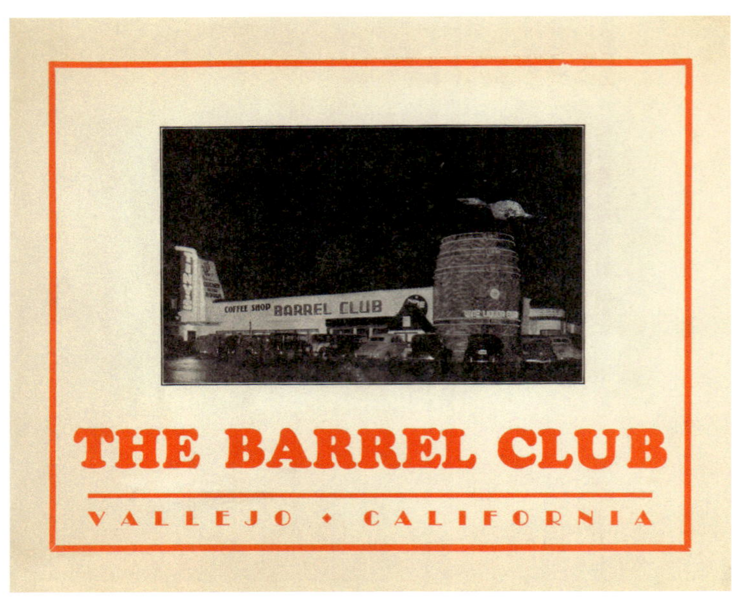

COFFEE SHOP BARREL CLUB
THE BARREL CLUB
VALLEJO • CALIFORNIA

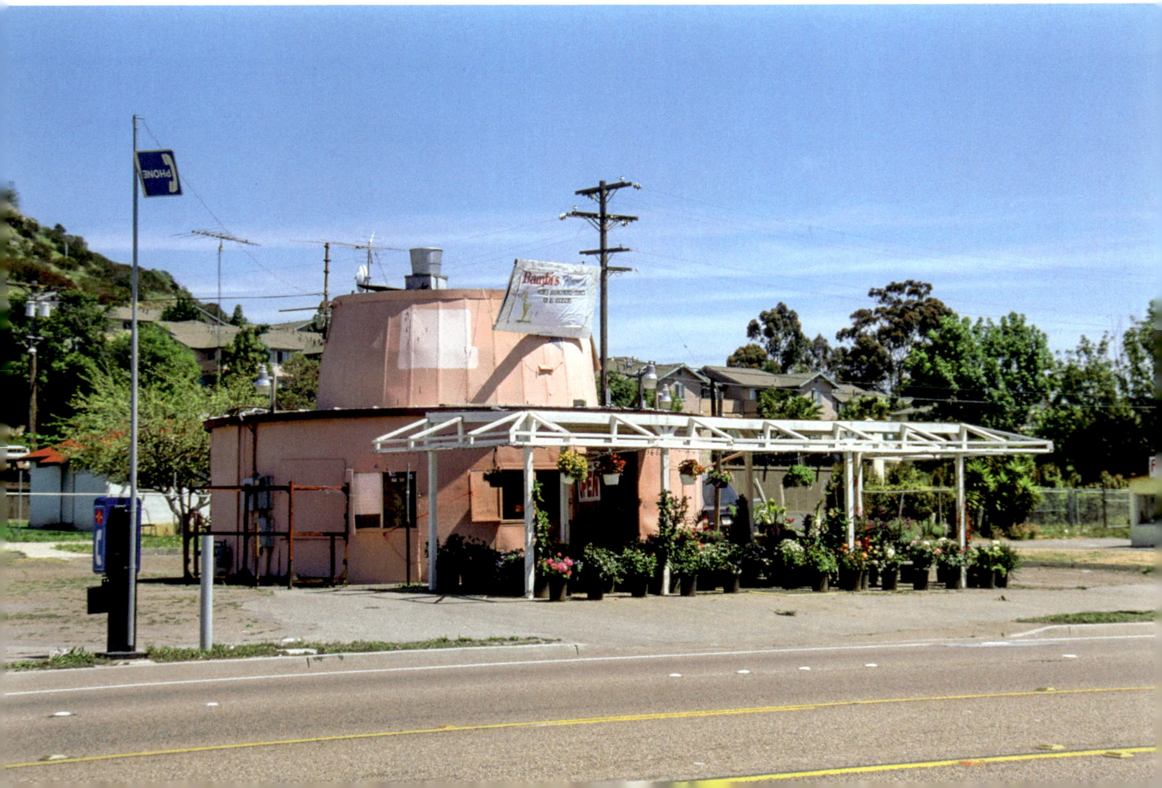
PHONE

OPPOSITE TOP
The Barrel Club souvenir photo holder, ca. 1944

OPPOSITE BOTTOM
Bambi's Flowers, Vista, 1999

RIGHT
Flower Barrel, University and Fairmount Avenues, San Diego, 1979

BELOW
Rodolfo's Taco Shop, San Diego, 1992

The BARREL
6425 San Fernando Rd.
GLENDALE, CALIF.

OPPOSITE
The Barrel matchcover, ca. 1927

RIGHT
Barrel Diner, Los Angeles, 1934

BELOW
Barrel Inn, 1525 North San Fernando Road, Glendale, ca. 1927

ABOVE
Beany's Drive-In, Pacific Coast Highway and Ximeno Avenue, Long Beach, 1952

OPPOSITE TOP
Benham's Brownie Cone, Fresno, ca. 1927

OPPOSITE BOTTOM
Bear Tree, 1240 South Beach Boulevard, Anaheim, ca. 1983

FOLLOWING SPREAD
Betsy Ann Ice Cream and Candy, Los Angeles, ca. 1929

Benham's
Benham's
BROWNIE
CONE
Benham's
BROWNIE
CONE

ICE CREAM & CANDIES
Betsy Ann
fancy
ICE CREAM & CANDIES.

ICE CREAM & CANDIES
Betsy An
fancy
ICE CREAM & CANDIE
GOOD OLD
EASTSIDE
THE PERFECT BREW
WE SERVE COLD DRINKS of all Kinds

THIS PAGE
Big Cone, Pacific Coast Highway, Laguna Beach, ca. 1933

OPPOSITE
Big Cone, Los Angeles, ca. 1932

LEFT
Big Cone advertisement, 1931

BELOW
Big Cone, Los Angeles, ca. 1931

OPPOSITE
McCorvey Locksmith,
607 West Manchester Avenue,
Los Angeles, 1980

McCORVEY
LOCKSMITH
Pregnancy Problem?
Call West Coast Medical Group at
INGLEWOOD HOSPITAL
674-5971
KEYS MADE HERE
607
Phone
CLOSED
Locksmith
PARKING ONLY
ALL OTHERS WILL BE TOWED AWAY AT OWNERS EXPENSE...
L.A.M.C. 80.74-1

DALE'S
DONUT'S
ATLANTIC AVE
OPEN

OPPOSITE
Dale's Donuts, 15904 Atlantic Avenue, Los Angeles, 2000

RIGHT
Kindle's Donuts, Century Boulevard at Normandie Avenue, Los Angeles, 2000

BELOW
Randy's Donuts, 805 West Manchester Boulevard, Los Angeles, ca. 2005

FOLLOWING SPREAD
The Donut Hole, La Puente, ca. 1985

DONU
"IT'S TH
ENTRANCE
DONUT LAN

HE
T HOLE
QUALITY"

ABOVE
Big Fireplace, 5837 Washington Boulevard, Los Angeles, 1927. Owner: Nat Goldstein

BELOW
Giant Orange, San Joaquin Valley, 1934

ABOVE
Big Orange, ca. 1964
RIGHT
Big Orange, ca. 1929

BELOW
Big Orange, California Citrus State Historic Park entrance, Riverside, 1995

OPPOSITE TOP
Binoculars Building, 340 Main Street, Venice, ca. 1991. Architect: Frank Gehry. Artists: Claes Oldenburg and Coosje van Bruggen

OPPOSITE BOTTOM
Big Golden Orange Wagon, 1250 North Western Avenue, Los Angeles, 1930

THE ORANGE WAGON
ORANGE WAGON
Carrying absolutely pure ORANGE JUICE and highest grade ICE CREAM.
Passes your door TWICE DAILY.
WATCH FOR THE CAR WITH THE BIG GOLDEN ORANGE
LISTEN FOR ITS BUGLE CHIMES
PHONE REQUEST WILL BRING SPECIAL DELIVERY
ORANGE WAGON CO.
HEMPSTEAD 4320
1250 NO. WESTERN AVE.

LEFT
Big Red Piano advertisement, ca. 1931

BELOW
Big Red Piano, 2251 Venice Boulevard, Los Angeles, ca. 1977. Architect: Frank Gaw

OPPOSITE
Big Red Piano, 2251 Venice Boulevard, Los Angeles, ca. 1930. Architect: Frank Gaw

DATES
DIRECT
FROM
OUR GARDENS

LACK TENT
DATES
DIRECT
OUR GARDENS

PREVIOUS SPREAD
Black Tent, South Palm Canyon Drive, Palm Springs, 1937

BELOW
Noah's Ark, U.S. 101, Leucadia, ca. 1945. Owners: Ed and Glenetta Barker

OPPOSITE TOP
S.S. Castle Rock, Smith River, ca. 1951

OPPOSITE BOTTOM
Hermosa Ship Club, ca. 1930

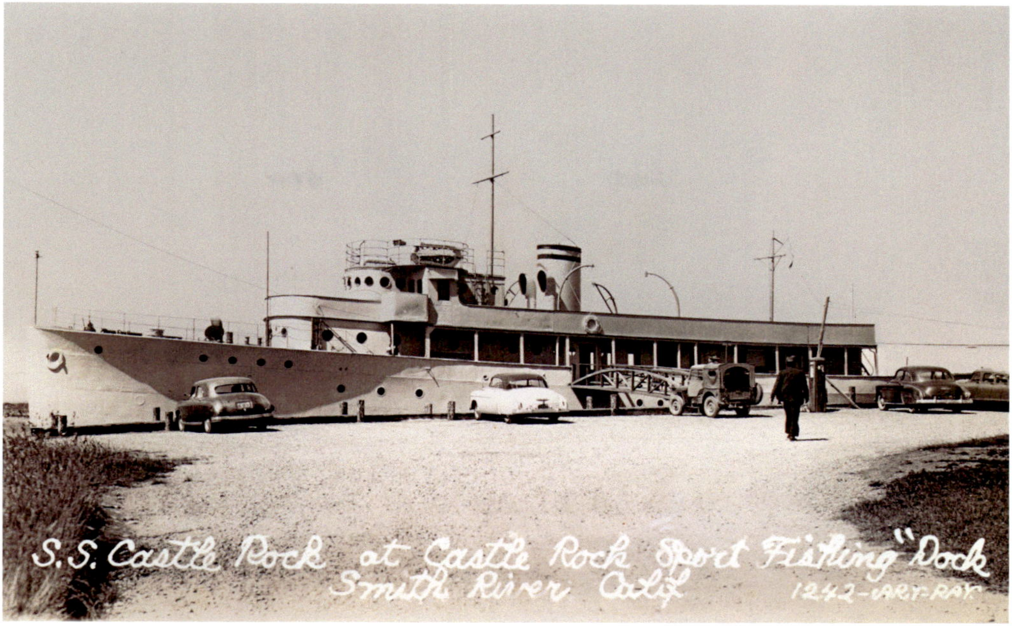
S.S. Castle Rock at Castle Rock Sport Fishing "Dock
Smith River Calif
1242-ART-RAY

HERMOSA SH
CLUB

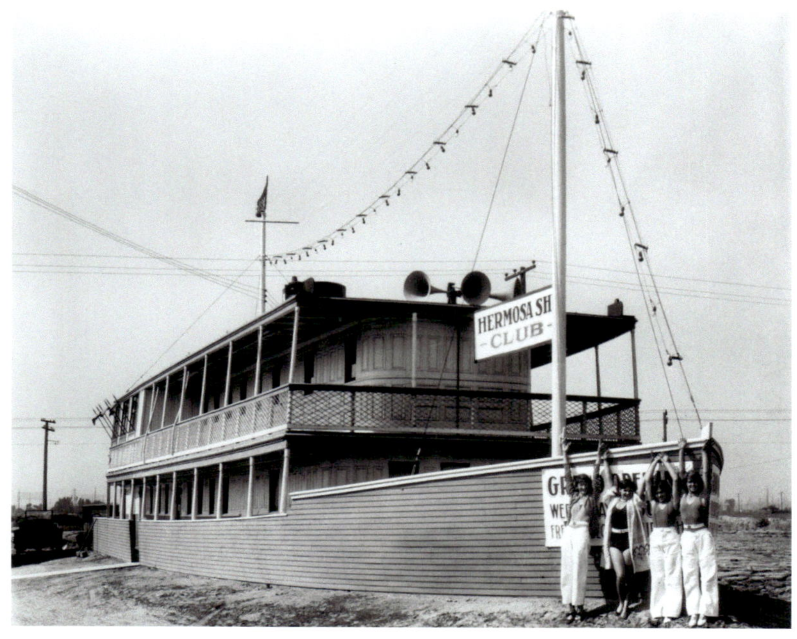

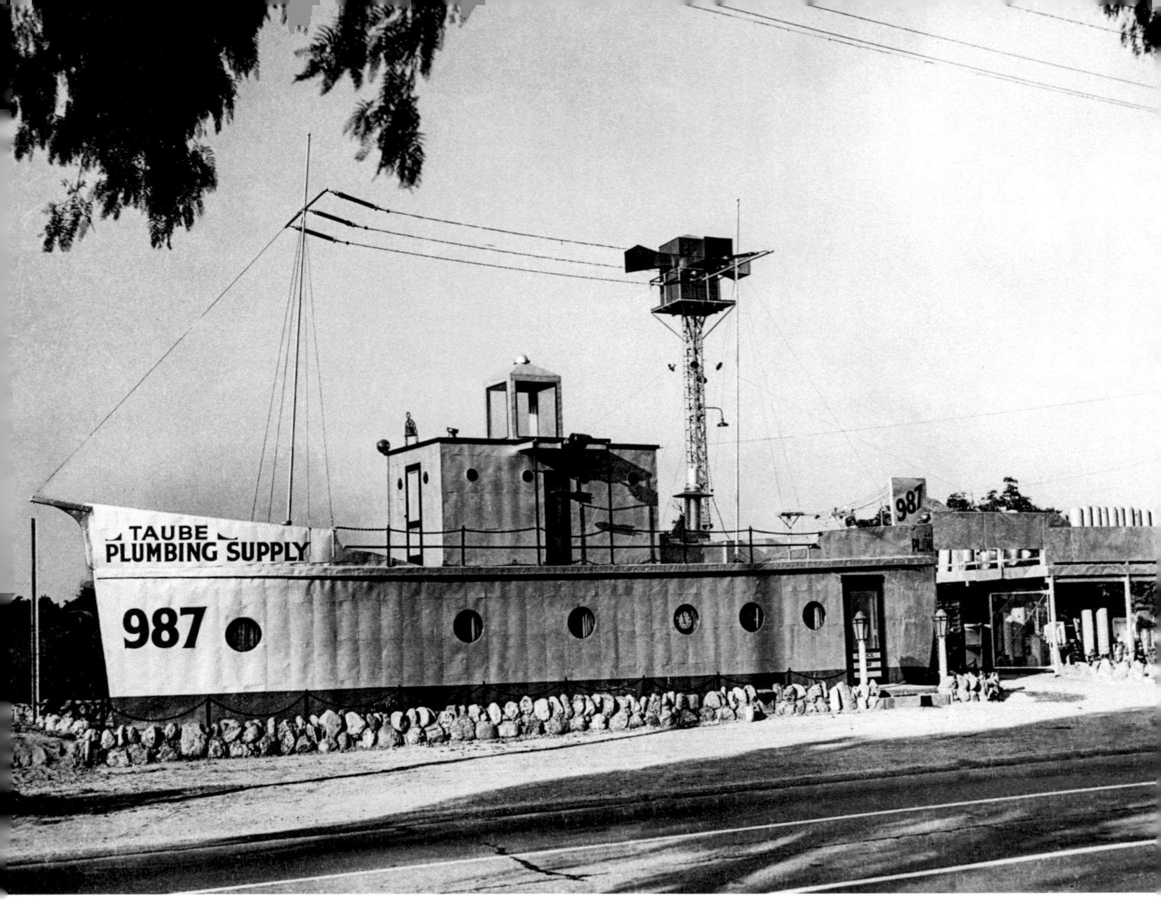
TAUBE
PLUMBING SUPPLY
987
987

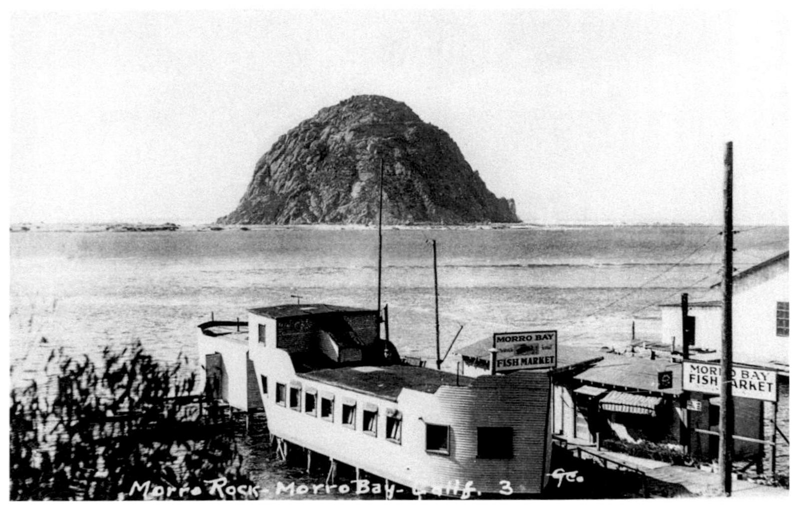

MORRO BAY
FISH MARKET
MORRO BAY
FISH MARKET
Morro Rock - Morro Bay - Calif. 3

OPPOSITE TOP
Taube Plumbing, Los Angeles, ca. 1927
OPPOSITE BOTTOM
Fish Market and Ship Café, Morro Bay, ca. 1926
ABOVE
Showboat, ca. 1935

BELOW

Arden Farms, 1900 West Slauson Avenue, Los Angeles, 1932

OPPOSITE

Chianti bottle, Italian Swiss Colony Vineyard, Asti, ca. 1929

ASTI
ITALIAN SWISS COLONY
CALIFORNIA
TIPO
WHITE WINE

LEFT
Renault Champagne statue, ca. 1940

BELOW
The Real Thing, 11702 Ventura Boulevard, Studio City, ca. 1976

OPPOSITE TOP
Giant bottle, 365 South Mount Vernon Avenue, San Bernardino, 1979

OPPOSITE BOTTOM
Sanitary Gold Seal Dairy Co. postcard, ca. 1912

Poplar
Mt. Vernon

SANITARY GOLD SEAL DAIRY CO.
SANITARY GOLD SEAL DAIRY CO.
SANITARY GOLD SEAL DAIRY CO.

EAT IN THE HAT
The Brown Derby

MUTUAL

PREVIOUS SPREAD
The Brown Derby, 3427 Wilshire Boulevard, Los Angeles, 1930

LEFT
The Brown Derby table tent, ca. 1929

BELOW AND OPPOSITE
The Brown Derby, 3427 Wilshire Boulevard, Los Angeles, ca. 1930

Desmond's
FOUR SONS
FRIGIDAIRE
Palos Verdes Estates

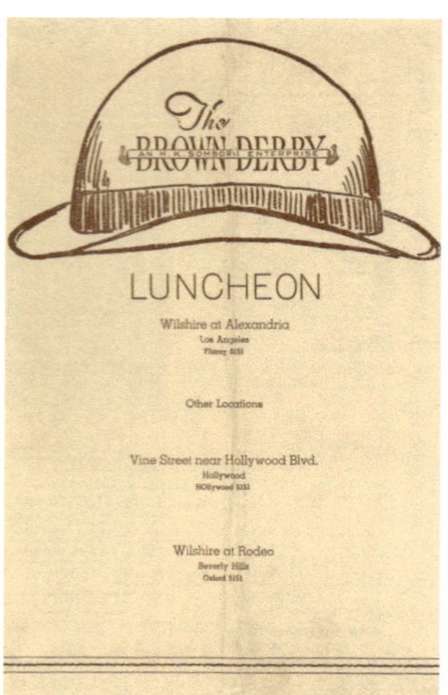


LEFT
The Brown Derby napkin, ca. 1942

RIGHT
The Brown Derby menu, 1936

BELOW
The Brown Derby opening, 3427 Wilshire Boulevard, Los Angeles, 1926

OPPOSITE
The Brown Derby gift catalog, ca. 1948

The
BROWN DERBY
HOLLYWOOD · CALIFORNIA
The BROWN DERBY
The Brown Derby
The Brown Derby Restaurant
Presents
Distinctive Gifts and Fine Foods

Lindgren & Swinerton Inc.
BUILDERS

OPPOSITE
The Brown Derby construction,
3377 Wilshire Boulevard,
Los Angeles, 1936

BELOW
The Brown Derby,
3377 Wilshire Boulevard,
Los Angeles, 1954

BELOW
Al's Coffee Shop, 4541 Eagle Rock Boulevard, Los Angeles, ca. 1930

OPPOSITE TOP
Al's Coffee Shop, 4541 Eagle Rock Boulevard, Los Angeles, ca. 1930

OPPOSITE BOTTOM
The Bucket, 4541 Eagle Rock Boulevard, Los Angeles, ca. 1979

AL'S COFFEE SHOP
ONE SPECIAL
Hot Plate Lunch
DAILY

Home Made
ERS
The Bucket
4541

TAMALE
ICE CREAM
1153
TOASTED SANDWICH
15¢
45¢ QT
25¢ PT
5¢
Coca-Cola

OPPOSITE
Bulldog Inn, 1153 Valley Boulevard, Rosemead, ca. 1934

ABOVE
Bulldog Inn, 1153 East Valley Boulevard, Rosemead, ca. 1939

RIGHT
Bulldog Inn, 1153 East Valley Boulevard, Rosemead, ca. 1930

LEFT
Cabazon Dinosaur, ca. 1964.
Designer: Claude Bell

BELOW AND OPPOSITE
Cabazon Dinosaur, ca. 1993.
Designer: Claude Bell

ABOVE
Cabot's Old Indian Pueblo, Desert Hot Springs, ca. 1945. Owner: Cabot Yerxa

LEFT
Calmos service station, 4982 Hollywood Boulevard, 1932

OPPOSITE
Calpet service station, 3237 Wilshire Boulevard, Los Angeles, ca. 1928. Architect: Roland E. Coate

CALPET

WILSHIRE
WILSHIRE
GREEN T CAFE
TEXACO

TEXACO
TEXACO
ETHYL
ere!
TEXACO ETHYL
is here!
GASOLINE
TEXACO
MOTOR OIL
TEXACO
16½

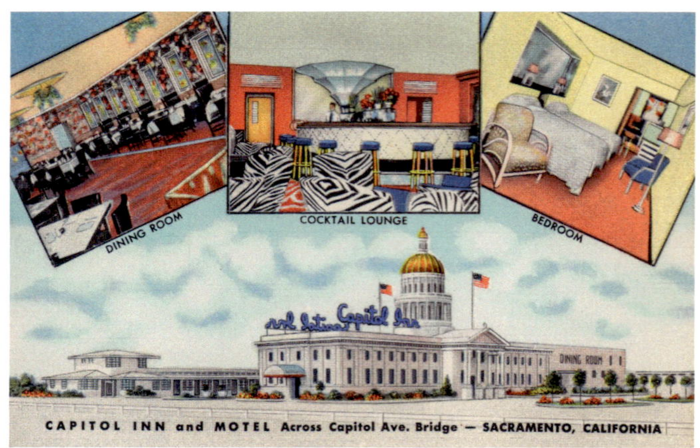


PREVIOUS SPREAD
Calpet service station, 3237 Wilshire Boulevard, Los Angeles, 1930

LEFT
Capitol Inn postcard, 1951

BELOW
Capitol Inn, U.S. 40 and U.S. 99, Sacramento, 1948

TOP
Carl's Jr., 2025 East Katella Avenue, Anaheim, 1999

BOTTOM
Ray L. Hommes,
828 South Robertson Boulevard,
Los Angeles, ca. 1927

BELOW
Castle Sans Souci, Franklin and Argyle Avenues, Hollywood, ca. 1918. Owner: Dr. Alfred Schloesser

OPPOSITE TOP
Tiree Castle, 414 Grand Avenue, Alhambra, ca. 1929. Owner: Alex McClean

OPPOSITE BOTTOM
Gunther Castle, Long Beach, 1920

DROP INTO
Gunther Castle
REAL-ESTATE
W 23RD ST

63

Castle San Souci, Franklin Avenue at Argyle Avenue, Hollywood, 1908. Owner: Dr. Alfred Schloesser

LEFT
Hamel's, 704 Ventura Place, San Diego, 2009

BELOW
Terraform Industries, 3320 San Fernando Road, Burbank, ca. 1989

OPPOSITE TOP
Castle City Grill, 82530 Highway 111, Indio, 2000

OPPOSITE BOTTOM
King's Castle, Toluca Lake, 1989

Castle City GRILL

KING'S CASTLE
STEAKS
SEAFOOD
KING'S CASTLE
RESTAURANT
TOLUCA LAKE
FOR SALE

LEFT
Eads Castle, 828 South Robertson Boulevard, Los Angeles, 1945

BELOW
Cave, 3303 Cahuenga Boulevard West, Los Angeles, 1931

OPPOSITE
The Castle matchcover, ca. 1945

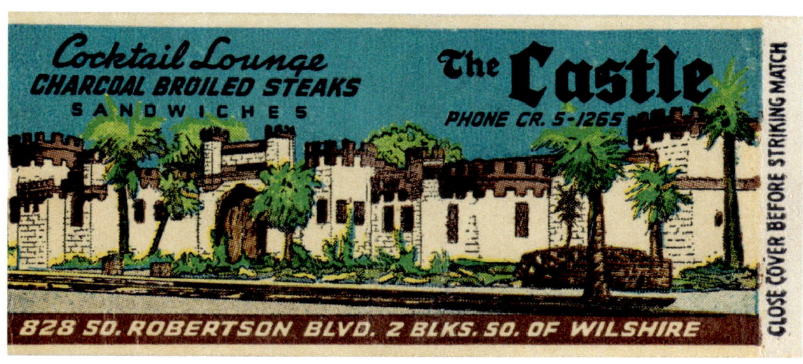

Cocktail Lounge
CHARCOAL BROILED STEAKS
SANDWICHES
The Castle
PHONE CR. 5-1265
828 SO. ROBERTSON BLVD. 2 BLKS. SO. OF WILSHIRE
CLOSE COVER BEFORE STRIKING MATCH

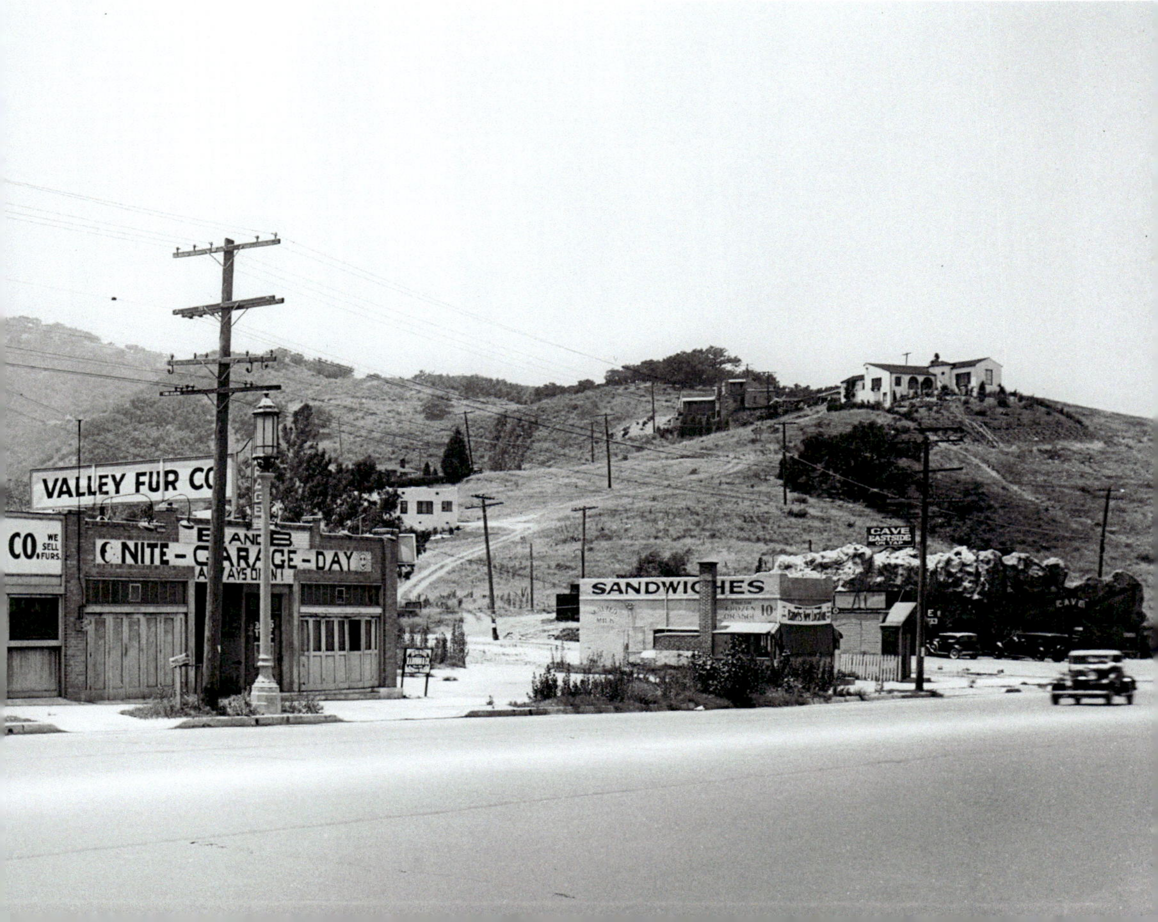
VALLEY FUR CO
CO. WE SELL FURS.
NITE - GARAGE - DAY
SANDWICHES
CAVE
EASTSIDE ON TAP

GET THE
CHILI BOWL
HABIT!
CHILI BOWL
BARBU-CATED STEAKS SPAGHETTI
SIZE
" AN INSTITUTION
BUILT THRU MERIT "

OPPOSITE AND ABOVE RIGHT
Chili Bowl matchcover, ca. 1935

ABOVE LEFT
Chili Bowl, 3012 Crenshaw Boulevard, Los Angeles, ca. 1937. Owner: Arthur Whizin

RIGHT
Chili Bowl, Los Angeles, ca. 1933

FOLLOWING SPREAD
Chili Bowl, 5081 Whittier Boulevard, Los Angeles, ca. 1933

AND NOW The 4TH
CHILI BOWL
OUR OWN TAMALES GRILLBURGERS
SIZE
GEN CONT.
JM LAMB
PA 0182

BEER

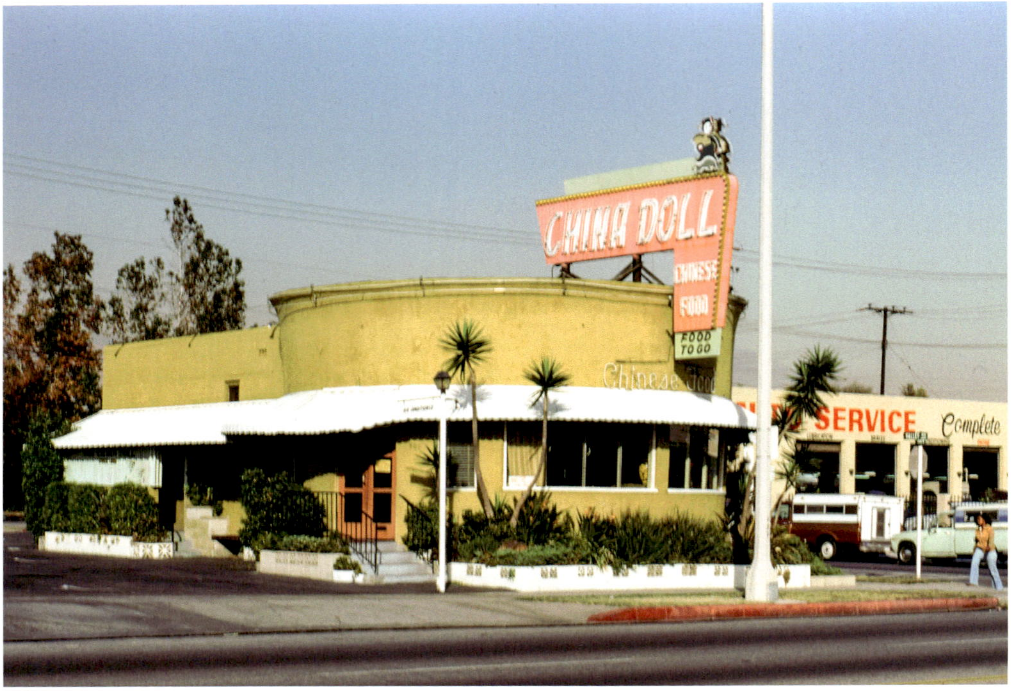
CHINA DOLL
CHINESE FOOD
FOOD TO GO
SERVICE
Complete

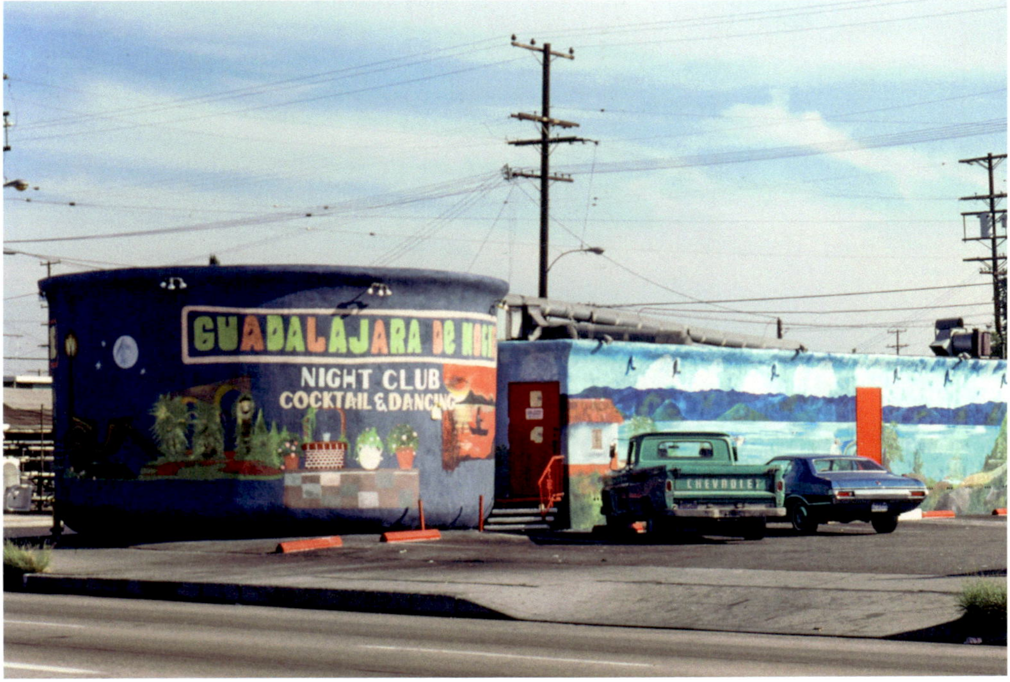
NIGHT CLUB
COCKTAIL & DANCING
CHEVROLET

OPPOSITE TOP
China Doll, 501 Valley Boulevard, Alhambra, 1979

OPPOSITE BOTTOM
Guadalajara de Noche Night Club, 2228 East Florence Avenue, Walnut Park, 1979

RIGHT
Round House, 12244 Pico Boulevard, Los Angeles, 1971

BELOW
Mr. Cecil's Ribs, 12244 Pico Boulevard, Los Angeles, 2006

Sensational ICE CREAM PRODUCTIONS
PUNCH & JUDY
ICE CREAM PARLORS

"AN - INSTITUTION - BUILT - THRU - MERIT"

GENERAL OFFICE
3614 W. Jefferson Blvd.

*Location of Bowls*

| | |
|---|---|
| 3012 Crenshaw Boulevard LOS ANGELES | 1401 North Atlantic Blvd. LONG BEACH |
| 2228 East Florence Avenue HUNTINGTON PARK | 111 North Fairfax HOLLYWOOD |
| 801 North La Brea HOLLYWOOD | 4351 South Figueroa Street LOS ANGELES |
| 5061 Whittier Boulevard BELVEDERE | 2453 Fletcher Drive LOS ANGELES |
| 3668 Beverly Boulevard LOS ANGELES | 1601 East Anaheim WILMINGTON |

*The Objective to Which We Strive Is—*

**FAST COURTEOUS SERVICE**

*We Will Greatly Appreciate Your Reporting to Our Office Any Failure to Live Up to These Principles . . .*

## CHILI BOWL MENU and GUEST CHECK

| ENTREES | |
|---|---|
| Size (Grilled Steak Chili - Beans) | .25 |
| Spaghetti Size (Grilled Steak Spaghetti) | .35 |
| Tamale & Chili | .30 |
| Tamale & Chili Con Carne | .35 |
| Tamale-Chili Beans | .40 |
| Spaghetti | .30 |
| Spaghetti Texas Beans | .40 |
| Chili Straight (Con Carne) | .25 |
| Chili Beans (Con Carne) | .25 |
| Chili Beans | .20 |
| Chicken Ravioli Special | .35 |
| Enchilada Special | .35 |
| Grillburger Steak Plain | .25 |
| Grillburger Steak Chili | .30 |
| Grillburger Steak Chili Beans | .35 |
| Egg Royal Plain | .30 |
| Egg Royal Chili | .35 |
| Egg Royal Chili Beans | .40 |
| Gr. Round Steak Potatoes | .35 |
| Ham Omelette | .40 |
| Cheese Omelette | .40 |
| Plain Omelette | .35 |
| Ham & Eggs | .40 |
| 2 Eggs Fried or Scrambled | .25 |
| Cold-Plate Pot. Salad (Summer Months) | .30 |
| EXTRA ITEMS | |

| SANDWICHES | |
|---|---|
| Cold Ham W | .15 |
| Fried Ham W | .15 |
| Cheese W | .15 |
| Egg W | .15 |
| *Above If Toasted* | .05 |
| Grillburger Sandwich | .15 |
| Grillburger Sand. Cheese | .20 |
| Melted Cheese W | .20 |
| Special Club W | .20 |
| Ground Steak Sand. W | .25 |
| Ham and Egg Sand. W | .25 |
| **DRINKS** | |
| Coffee Real Cr. per cup | .05 |
| Tea | .10 |
| Hot Chocolate | .10 |
| Buttermilk | .10 |
| Milk | .10 |
| Soda 12 oz. Bottle | .10 |
| Kava Kola (Fountain) | .05 |
| Bottled Beer | .10 |
| " " | .15 |
| Canned Beer | .20 |
| **DESSERTS** | |
| Pie (our own) | .10 |
| Pie in a Bowl (cream) | .15 |
| Tomato Juice | .15 |
| Soup | .15 |
| Roll (Franco) | .05 |
| Roll - Butter | .10 |

| CHECK NO. | WAITER NO. | |
|---|---|---|
| 00038 | A-B-C-D | TOTAL |

PLEASE PAY AT YOUR SEAT - THANK YOU

OUR CHILI BEANS ARE THE DECORATIONS OF A "SIZE" AS SERVED BY THE

CHILI BOWL

2228 East Florence
Near Sante Fe
Huntington Park
JEfferson 9603

801 North La Brea
Near Melrose Ave.
Hollywood
WYoming 9160

3012 Crenshaw Blvd.
Near Jefferson
Los Angeles
PArkway 9241

« ORDERS PUT UP TO TAKE OUT »

(over)

OPPOSITE
Punch & Judy menu, ca. 1948

ABOVE
Chili Bowl menu, ca. 1935

RIGHT
Chili Bowl business card, ca. 1933

***As colorful and romantic as Los Angeles is the***
**"CLIFF DWELLERS"**

•

It was conceived and founded in 1925 by a caterer who realized that cuisine and unusually good food in a unique atmosphere would attract a class of people who would appreciate the difference.

It is suggested that if you are looking for an evening of Real Fiesta "Whoopee" . . . one that the whole family will enjoy . . . you will visit California's unique restaurant at 3591 Beverly Boulevard.

**Here you will relax and listen to beautiful music and partake of food that you will happily remember.**

•

**CORT FOX'S**
# CLIFF DWELLERS
**CAFE**

3591 BEVERLY BLVD. DRexel 9567
LOS ANGELES

OPPOSITE
Cliff Dwellers Café advertisement, ca. 1931

ABOVE
Cliff Dwellers Café matchcover, 1929

RIGHT
Cliff Dwellers Café menu, ca. 1933

BELOW
Cliff Dwellers Café, 3591 Beverly Boulevard, Los Angeles, ca. 1925

CLIFF DWELLERS
CHICKEN · STEAK · SQUAB

SOUVENIR MENU

DINNERS

Chicken Dinner - - - $1.25
Jumbo Squab - - - - $1.25
Steak Dinner [N. Y. Cut] - $1.25
Chicken Livers Saute [full order] $1.25

The above orders include Shoe-string Potatoes, Corn Pones, Biscuits, Honey, Relish, Coffee, Tea or Milk

Special Club House Sandwich [after 10 p. m. only] - - $1.00
[Coffee, Tea or Milk Included]

SIDE ORDERS

Chicken Broth - - - - .25
Lettuce and Tomato Salad - .35
Chicken Livers Saute - - .40
Celery and Olives - - - .35

BEVERAGES

Canada Dry - - .50
Silver Fizz - - .50
White Rock - - .50
Eastside - - - .25

NO SERVICE LESS THAN ONE DOLLAR

3591 BEVERLY BOULEVARD
FOUR BLOCKS EAST OF VERMONT

DRexel 9567

Los Angeles, California

"Most Unique of Cafes"

CORTLAND S. FOX
Proprietor

MUSIC
ENTERTAINMENT

Open 5 p. m. to 2 a. m. daily
Sundays, 2 p. m. to 1 a. m.

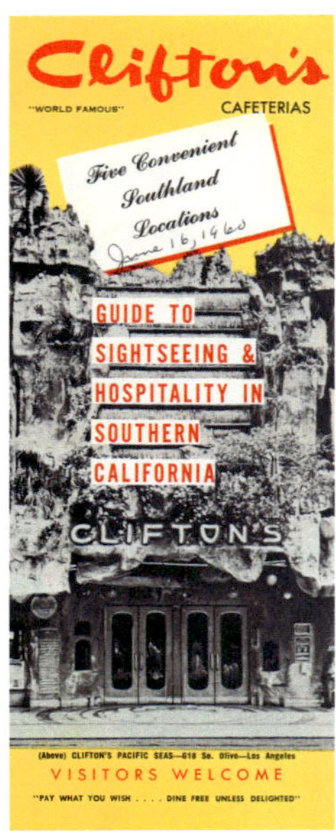


LEFT
Clifton's brochure, 1960

BELOW AND OPPOSITE TOP
Clifton's, 618 South Olive Street, Los Angeles, ca. 1935

OPPOSITE BOTTOM
Clifton's, 618 South Olive Street, Los Angeles, ca. 1950

YOUR SOUVENIR PHOTO FROM
Clifton's
Los Angeles, California
THE BROOKDALE
THE PACIFIC SEAS

BELOW
Clifton's, 618 South Olive Street, Los Angeles, ca. 1935

OPPOSITE TOP
Streamline Diner menu, 1938

OPPOSITE MIDDLE
The Club Car, Wilshire and San Vicente Boulevards, Los Angeles, ca. 1938. Owners: Alice Fay and Harry Sugarman

OPPOSITE BOTTOM
Cobb's Chicken House, Golden Gate International Exposition, 1939

FOLLOWING SPREAD
Coca-Cola Bottling Company, 1334 South Central Avenue, Los Angeles, ca. 1939. Architect: Robert V. Derrah

COOK'S STREAMDINER
STEAKS & CHOPS
COCKTAILS
6594

STEAKS CHOPS
STEAKS
THE CLUB CAR
FREE PARKING

COBB'S Famous CHICKEN HOUSE
½ FRIED CHICKEN
FRIED IN BUTTER
Southern Style...50¢
100 PER CENT CHICKEN TURNOVER 30¢
CHICKEN A LA KING 30¢
Pie or Cake 10¢ Tea 5¢
Coffee 5¢ Coca Cola 5¢
COBB'S Famous CHICKEN HOUSE
THE ONLY ORIGINAL CHICKEN HOUSE ON THE FAIR GROUNDS, TREASURE ISLAND, . . . . SAN FRANCISCO, CALIFORNIA

Coca-Cola

Coca-Cola Bottling Company

THE CUP
DRIVE IN

OPPOSITE
Coffee Cup, 8901 West Pico Boulevard, Los Angeles, ca. 1940

ABOVE
Coffee Cup, 8901 West Pico Boulevard, Los Angeles, ca. 1929

Coffee Pot, 7275 Beverly Boulevard, Los Angeles, ca. 1930

BEN-HUR
COFFEE
HOME MADE PIES
Fresh Peach 20
Eastern Pitted Cherry 15
FRENCH APPLE · PRUNE FLUFF
LEMON CHIFFON 15
FRESH
STRAWBERRY
ICE CREAM SODA 15¢ SUNDAE 20¢
MALTED MILK 20¢ MILK SHAKE 20¢
HOME MADE PIES
Fresh Peach 20
Eastern Pitted Cherry 15
FRENCH APPLE · PRUNE FLUFF
LEMON CHIFFON 15

OPPOSITE
Coffee Pot, 7275 Beverly Boulevard, Los Angeles, ca. 1930

RIGHT
Coffee Pot matchcover, ca. 1930

BELOW
Coffee Pot, 7275 Beverly Boulevard, Los Angeles, ca. 1936

ABOVE
Coffee Pot advertisement, Los Angeles, 1930

RIGHT
Cookie Jar, Los Angeles, ca. 1931

OPPOSITE
The Cream Can, Los Angeles, ca. 1928

FOLLOWING SPREAD
Crossroads of the World, 6671 Sunset Boulevard, Hollywood, ca. 1937

The CREAM CAN
"Cream of Dairy Products"
CREAM CAN
REAL CHURNED
Buttermilk 5¢
CREAM
Buttermilk
5¢
1411
EAST SIDE
COTTAGE CHEESE
ICE CREAM
BUTTER MILK
MILKS

CROSS
HOLLYWOODLAND
OPEN ABOUT NOVEMBER 15th
A. J. MATHIEU CO.
GROCERS • IMPORTERS
• GIFT BASKETS FOR ALL OCCASIONS
• FRESH CAVIAR
• DELICACIES
• FINE WINES & LIQUEURS

BARBER OF Seville
Billie's
Billie's

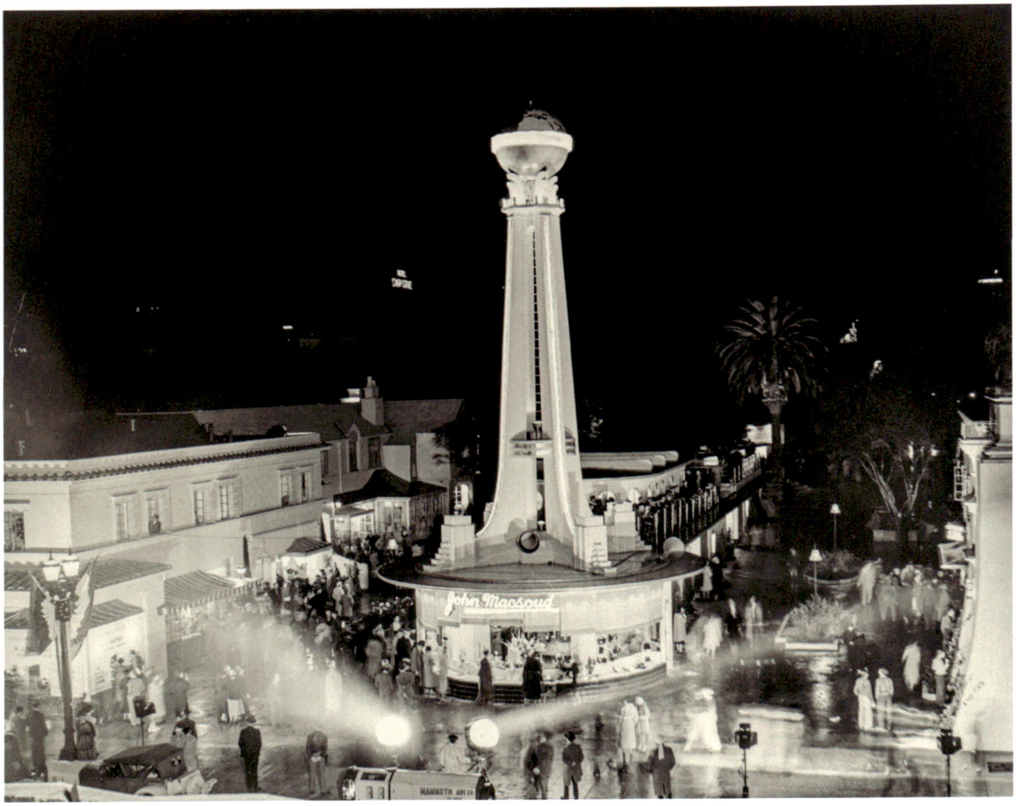
John Macsoud

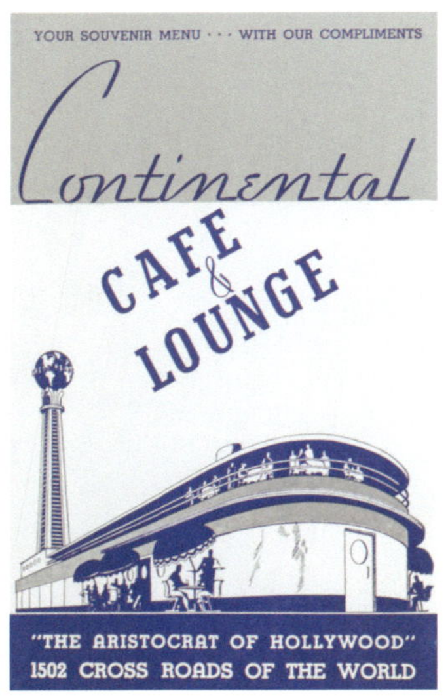

YOUR SOUVENIR MENU · · · WITH OUR COMPLIMENTS
Continental
CAFE & LOUNGE
"THE ARISTOCRAT OF HOLLYWOOD"
1502 CROSS ROADS OF THE WORLD

OPPOSITE TOP
Crossroads of the World opening, 6671 Sunset Boulevard, Hollywood, ca. 1936

OPPOSITE BOTTOM
Crossroads of the World menu, ca. 1938

THIS PAGE
Crossroads of the World, 6671 Sunset Boulevard, Hollywood, ca. 1938

LEFT AND OPPOSITE
Crossroads of the World, 6671 Sunset Boulevard, Hollywood, 1936

BELOW
Crossroads of the World advertisement, 1937

*The Smart Shopping Center On Busy Sunset Boulevard*

The CROSSROADS OF THE WORLD brings to you such an ideal location — in the HEART of HOLLYWOOD, one of the busiest shopping centers in the world! It offers to the real merchant an opportunity to place himself in the midst of a group dealing in the interesting things of all lands, and yet away from the distractions of modern traffic.

Here in one artistic group of shops and studios, in a setting of natural beauty, will be displayed the goods and services of the world. Here at the very core of one of the busiest shopping districts in the world, one can step into the quiet calm of Old World streets, away from the rush and confusion of traffic, and shop to the heart's content!

The CROSS ROADS of the WORLD

**THE CROSSROADS OF THE WORLD**

**IN HOLLYWOOD + 6665 SUNSET BOULEVARD**

BARBER OF Seville

WORLD

BARBEQUED HAM
UNDER NEW MANAGEMENT
HOT LUNCH
SPOON
DEPOT
SUNFREZE
ICE CREAM
CUP & SPOON
5¢ PER GLASS
"A BETTER
MALTED MILK"
DRINKS

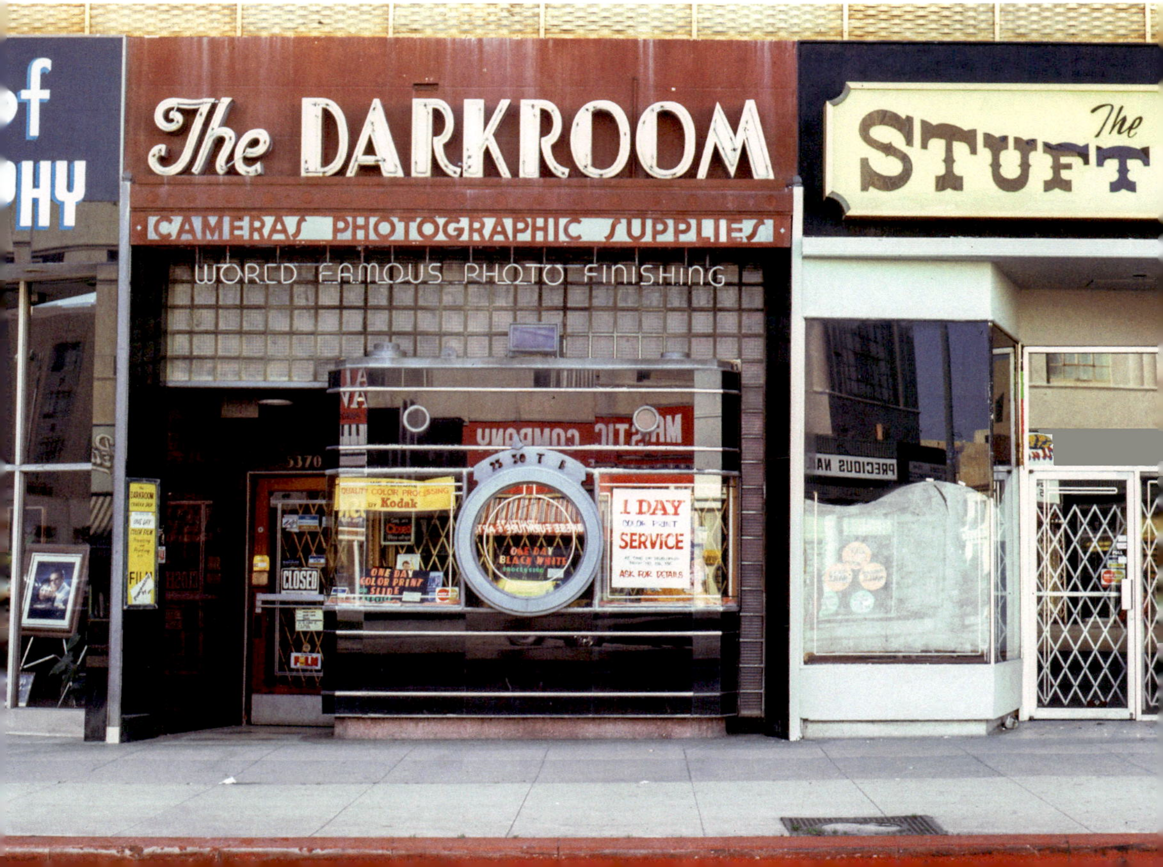

OPPOSITE TOP
Cup and Spoon, Los Angeles, 1931

OPPOSITE BOTTOM
The Darkroom, 5370 Wilshire Boulevard, Los Angeles, 1980

ABOVE
Dive!, 10250 Santa Monica Boulevard, Century City, 1994. Owners: Steven Spielberg and Jeffrey Katzenberg

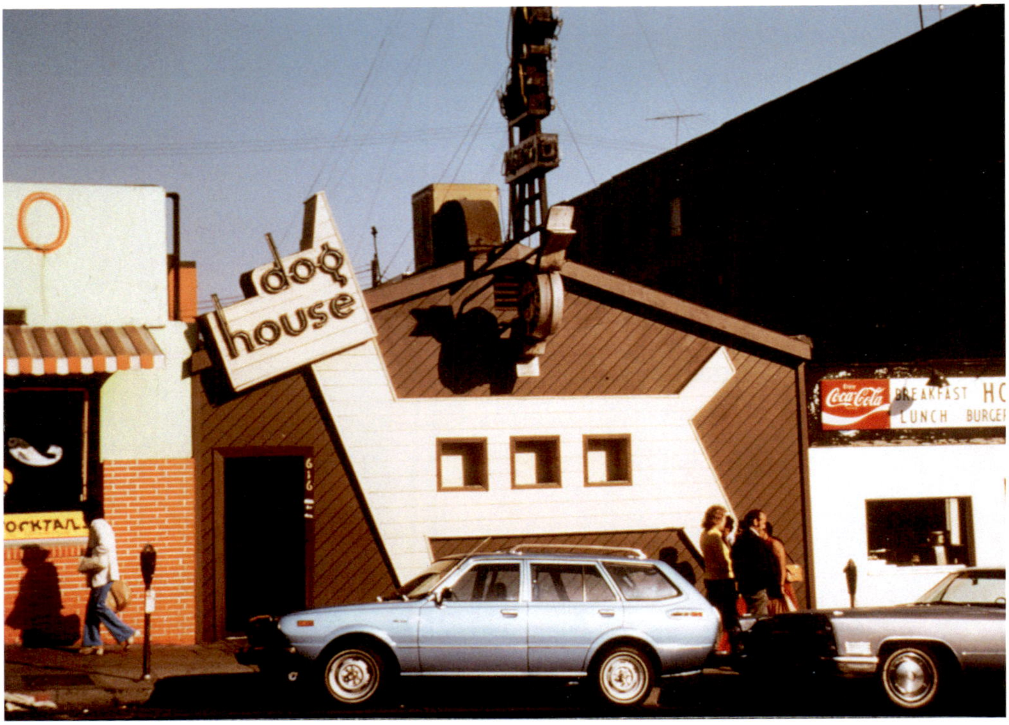
dog house
616
Coca-Cola
BREAKFAST
LUNCH
BURGER

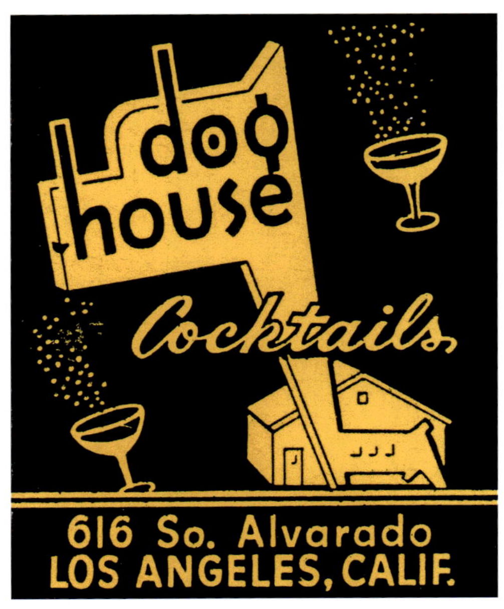

dog house
Cocktails
616 So. Alvarado
LOS ANGELES, CALIF.

PREVIOUS SPREAD
Walt Disney Studios, 500 South Buena Vista Street, Burbank, 1990. Architect: Michael Graves

OPPOSITE TOP
Dog House, 616 South Alvarado Street, Los Angeles, ca. 1983

OPPOSITE BOTTOM
Dog House matchcover, ca. 1957

BELOW
The Dog House, Melrose Avenue and La Cienega Boulevard, Los Angeles, ca. 1977

The DUGOUT
6157
DUGOUT
FRENCH DIP
SANDWICHES

OPPOSITE
The Dugout, 6157 Whittier Boulevard, Montebello, ca. 1927

BELOW
Edison Field, Anaheim, 1999

BELOW
*The Ten Commandments* movie set, Guadalupe-Nipomo Dunes, ca. 1923

OPPOSITE TOP
Whiting-Mead advertising pavilion, Panama-California Exposition, San Diego, ca. 1915

OPPOSITE BOTTOM
Amen-Ra Apartments advertisement, 542 North Alexandria Avenue, Hollywood, 1925

# CLOSE COMPLETES STRIKING NEW APARTMENT

*Egyptian Structure Called "Masterpiece" of Designing and Building*

*Amen-Ra Apartments, 542 North Alexandria; Mr. and Mrs. August J. Blot, Owners.*

## Another Exceptional CLOSE CREATION!

IT is not without pride that we present the newly completed $75,000 **AMEN-RA** apartment house at 542 North Alexandria Street, just finished for Mr. and Mrs. August J. Blot. And it gives us added satisfaction in that those associated with us, from the Hammond Lumber Company which furnished the rough lumber, to the artists who did the most delicate of finishing, have joined us in a true pride of accomplishment.

THE **AMEN-RA**, declared by critics one of the most perfect examples of Egyptian architecture in the West, was Close-designed and Close-bilt for the owners. Mr. and Mrs. Blot, having just opened the structure to tenants, are so satisfied that they have just authorized this organization to design and construct another and larger income property.

*For years we have specialized in income property—and we handle everything for our clients: designing, building, furnishing, landscaping, and will finance if desired.*

All interested in income properties—or merely in distinctive and beautiful buildings—are invited to go out to 542 North Alexandria and inspect the AMEN-RA.

## J. M. CLOSE

241 North Western HEmpstead 2117

WE DESIGN! WE BUILD! WE FINANCE!

**The New AMEN-RA**

was completely fitted out by us with Special coil spring Murphy IN-A-DOOR beds.

**Southern Calif. Hardwood & Mfg. Co.**
Distributors
Sales Room 1807 So. Main St. Tel. WEstmore 5978

**Whiting-Mead Company**

Manufacturers and Jobbers of Building Materials exends congratulations to Mr. and Mrs. Blot on the completion of their beautiful new apartment house for which we furnished the finished lumber.

Main Offices 415 East 9th St. Yard & Mill 2045 E. Vernon Ave.
C. S. OWENS, Manager Lumber Dept.

Originally designed Egyptian ornamental iron work was chosen by J. M. Close for the AMEN-RA, and made to order by us.

**Winter Iron Works**
240 W. Manchester THornwall 4137

NOACK built-in ironing boards have been exclusively used in CLOSE-BILT apartments for the last 5 years.

**Noack Ironing Board Co.**
1040 S. Broadway TRinity 8531

A perfected landscape is the proper setting for such a gem of architecture.

**Jean Guichot, Landscape Gardener**
49th and Figueroa AXridge 7219

LEFT
Egyptian Salt Water Swimming Club advertisement, 1925

BELOW
Dawson's Auto Repair, Stockton, 1981

OPPOSITE
Sphinx head, ca. 1923

ESQUIMAUX
VILLAGE

OPPOSITE
Esquimaux Village, Ocean Park, 1915. Designer/builder: John G. Beem

BELOW
Esquimaux Village, California Midwinter International Exposition, San Francisco, 1894

LEFT

Parker-Judge Co. decorators, 224 North Juanita Avenue, Los Angeles, ca. 1930. Architect: Earl LeMoine

BELOW

Tuck Box English Cake Shop and Tea Room, Carmel by the Sea, ca. 1927. Designer: Hugh Comstock

OPPOSITE

Tupper and Reed, 2271 Shattuck Avenue, Berkeley, ca. 1927. Architect: W. R. Yelland

English Cake Shop and Tea Room
Carmel by the Sea, Calif.

TUPPER
REED
MUSIC
SAYERS WOMEN

ABOVE
Hollywood Flower Pot,
1100 North Vine Street, 1930

OPPOSITE
The Freezer, 126 South El
Molino Avenue, Pasadena,
ca. 1927

REEZER
126
SAMARKAND
FRENCH SUPREME
ICE CREAM
S. EL MOLINO AVE

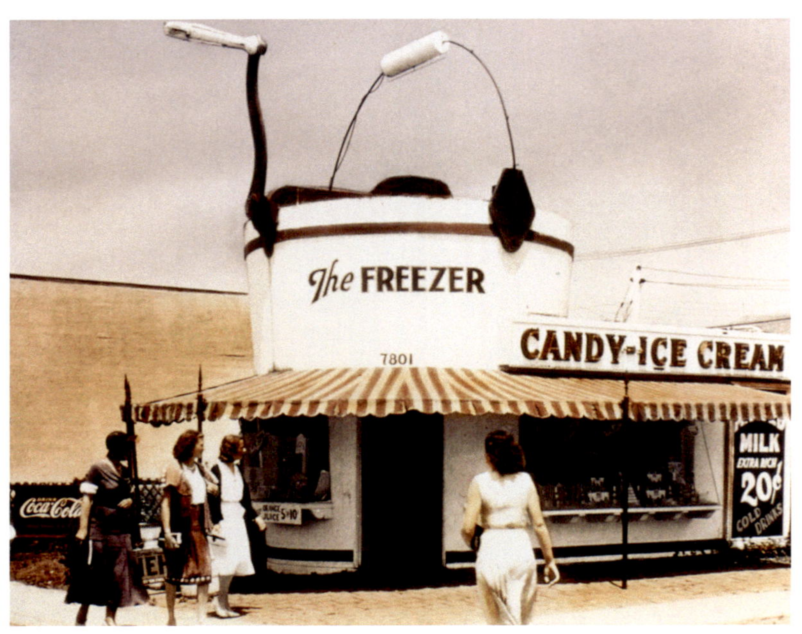

The FREEZER
7801
CANDY-ICE CREAM
MILK
EXTRA RICH
20¢
COLD DRINKS
Coca-Cola

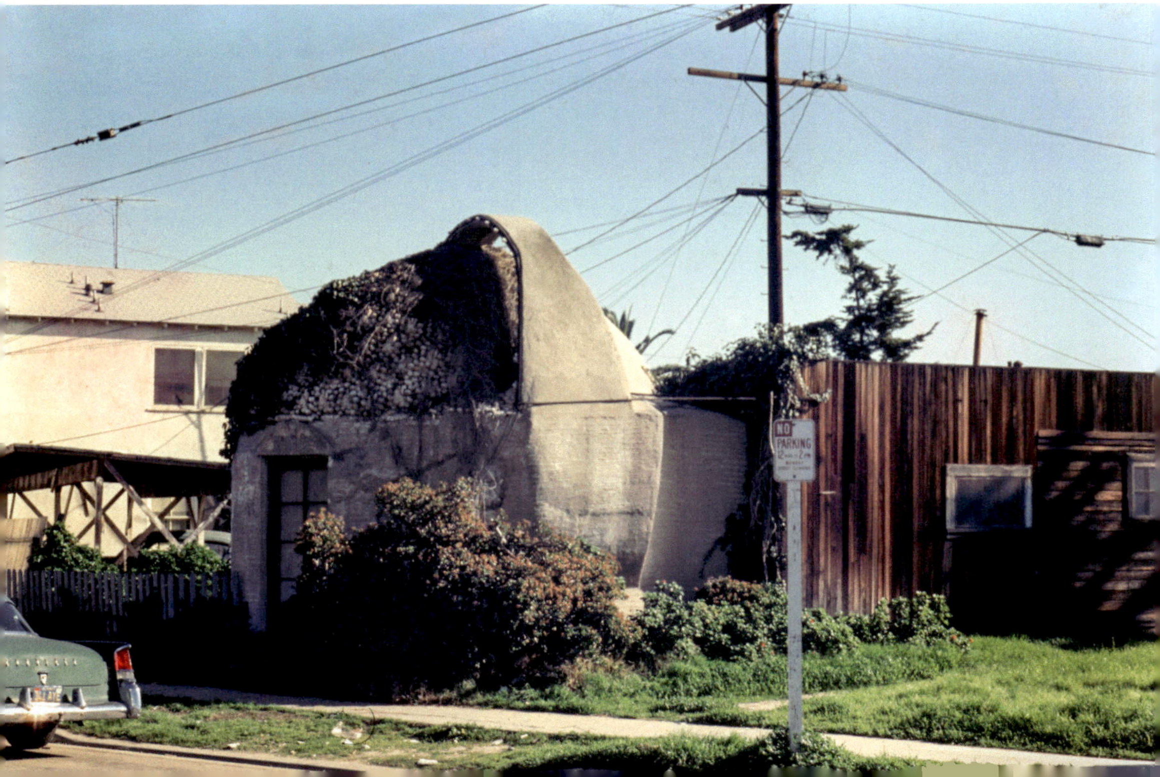
NO PARKING

OPPOSITE TOP
The Freezer, 7801 West Washington Boulevard, Los Angeles, ca. 1933

OPPOSITE BOTTOM
Fruit Basket, Los Angeles, 1974

BELOW
Fry's Electronics, 2311 North Hollywood Way, Burbank, 1997

ABOVE
Garden of Allah, Long Beach, ca. 1930

LEFT
Garden of Allah menu, ca. 1930

OPPOSITE TOP
Gay's Lion Farm, El Monte, ca. 1932

OPPOSITE BOTTOM
Gay's Lion Farm, Peck Road and Valley Boulevard, El Monte, ca. 1933

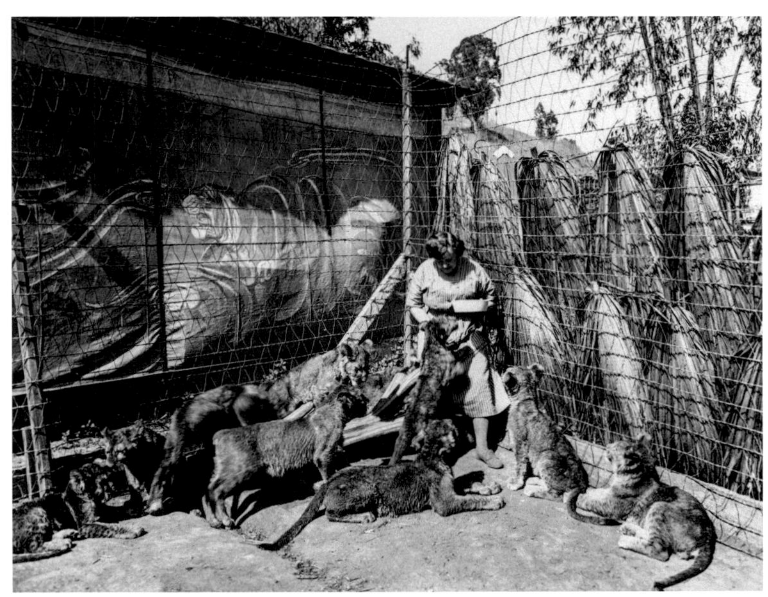

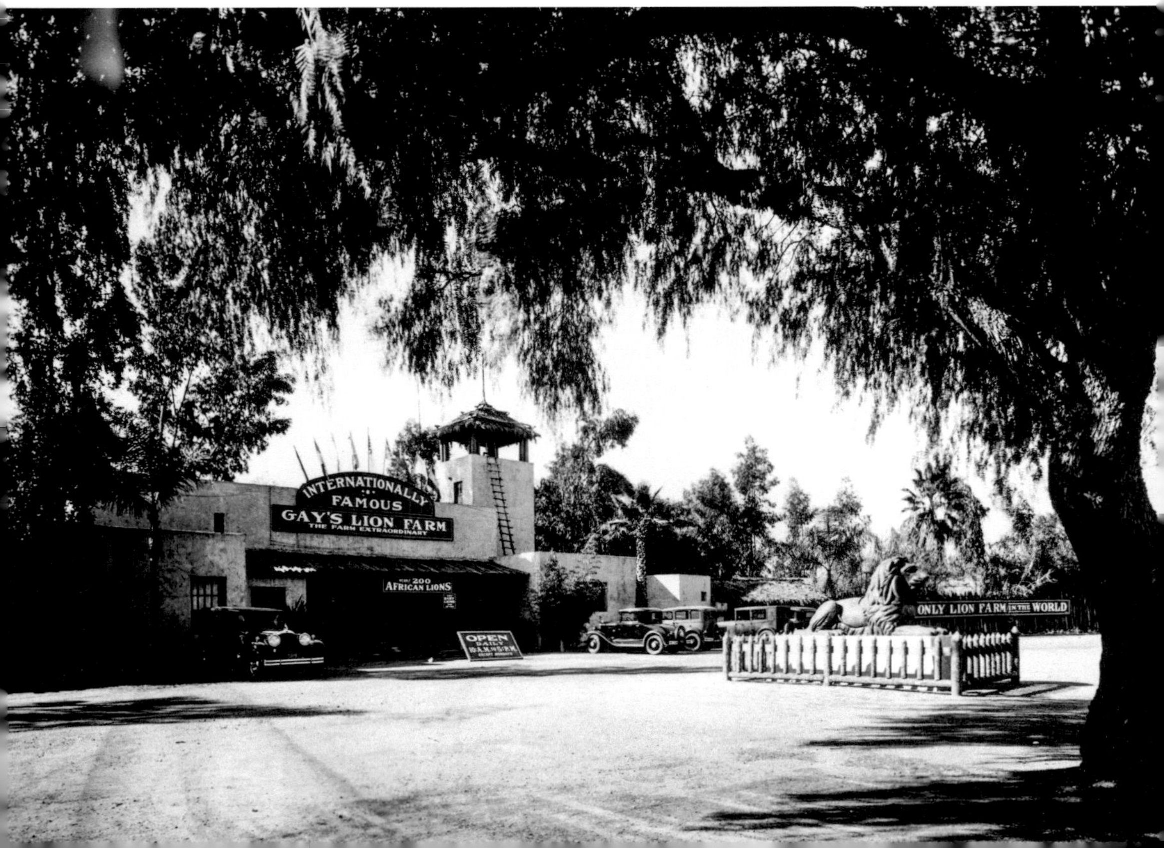
INTERNATIONALLY FAMOUS
GAY'S LION FARM
THE FARM EXTRAORDINARY
200
AFRICAN LIONS
OPEN DAILY
ONLY LION FARM IN THE WORLD

ABOVE AND BELOW
Gay's Lion Farm, Peck Road and Valley Boulevard, El Monte, ca. 1926

OPPOSITE
Gay's Lion Farm brochure, ca. 1926

Mrs. Gay and Numa, friends, beyond question

A Movie King

His Daily Dozen

He Dares You

100,000 Square Feet of Arenas

Thinking?

# An Educational Attraction You Will Never Forget

Blissful Moments

One of the main attractions at the Farm is the large number of baby Lions, some with their mothers and others being cared for by Mrs. Gay, who feeds them from an ordinary nursing bottle.

Some authorities on animal life have contended that Lions cannot be bred and reared in captivity, but this theory is exploded at Gay's Lion Farm, where magnificent specimens are raised in large numbers to supply the ever-increasing demand of circuses, zoos and amusement parks throughout the world. Animals far superior to those imported from the African Jungles can be seen here in a perfect state of health and contentment.

## Motion Picture Lions

Lions from this unique Farm have been shown throughout the World. People marvel and thrill at the scenes and wonder how it is done. You can see these same animals as they would pose before the camera. Meet "Numa"—the world's most valuable Lion, and "Slats"—the one that plays the heavy roles before the camera. It is something to know and be able to talk about.

A visit to this, the world's most unique Farm, will prove interesting, instructive and entertaining. Your questions are answered by one of the world's foremost authorities, a man who KNOWS Lions from a life of observation and experience in raising and training these monarchs of the Jungle.

Mr. Gay calls them by name. His skill and scientific understanding have enabled him to build this outstanding show place of America. It is his pleasure, joy and happiness. Visit the Lion Farm and gain a better appreciation of what this folder attempts to tell.

Complete your circle of California by arranging for a few hours' visit with these intelligent beasts and be able to converse on a subject that excites the admiration and interest of everyone. Tell people what you have seen, and know that nowhere else in the world is it possible to see these magnificent brutes as they are shown here.

THE ONLY LION FARM IN THE WORLD

Triumphant

To visit the great Southwest and not see Gay's Lion Farm, is like going to Egypt and not seeing the Pyramids. People of national and international repute, from all parts of the world, have visited this Farm and say it is one of the most interesting places they have ever seen.

BELOW
Bull Stops Here Barbecue, Visalia, 1998

OPPOSITE
George's Chicken, 3217 West Florence Avenue, Inglewood, ca. 1975

DINNERS
George's
GEORGE'S CHICKEN
3217

BELOW

Trees of Mystery Park, Redwood Highway, ca. 1950

OPPOSITE

Chicken Boy, 450 South Broadway, Los Angeles, 1979

CHICKEN BOY
LI-LING
ZENITH
JEWELRY

TONY'S
TRANSMISSION

CADILLAC
LINCOLN
Cadillac

OPPOSITE, CLOCKWISE FROM TOP LEFT
Golfer, Los Angeles, 1979

La Salsa man, Pacific Coast Highway, Malibu, 1988

Used car lot, Los Angeles, ca. 1978

Tony's Transmission, Los Angeles, ca. 1994

ABOVE
Jenkins Giant Muffler, Vista, 1999

Amir
353

OPPOSITE
Amir, 353 Rodeo Drive, Beverly Hills, 1993

RIGHT
Giant clam, Pismo Beach, 1979

BELOW
Prop from *Land of the Giants,* Universal Studios, Los Angeles, 1970

BELOW AND OPPOSITE
Girard Inn, Topanga Canyon and Ventura Boulevards, Woodland Hills, ca. 1937

FOLLOWING SPREAD
The Glacier, Crenshaw Boulevard, Los Angeles, 1928

GIRARD

MESA BARBECUE
PAN-GAS
SANDWICHES

WILSHIRE GASOLINE
5 93
5 93

Dedication
GRAUMAN'S CHINESE
THEATRE
HOLLYWOOD
WITH PREMIERE
CECIL B.
DE MILLE'S
"The
KING OF KINGS"

OPPOSITE
Grauman's Chinese Theatre program, 1927

RIGHT
Grauman's Chinese Theatre, 6925 Hollywood Boulevard, 1927

BELOW
Grauman's Chinese Theatre, 6925 Hollywood Boulevard, 1934

FOLLOWING SPREAD
Grauman's Chinese Theatre, 6925 Hollywood Boulevard, ca. 1927

CHINESE

SID GRAU
G

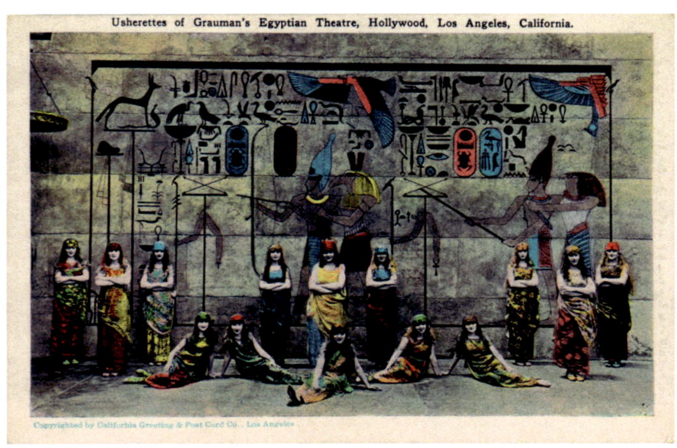


ABOVE
Grauman's Egyptian Theatre, 6712 Hollywood Boulevard, ca. 1924

LEFT
Grauman's Egyptian Theatre, ca. 1922

OPPOSITE
Grauman's Egyptian Theatre, 6712 Hollywood Boulevard, ca. 1922

LEFT
Green Mill Gardens advertisement, 1922

BELOW
Green Mill Gardens, Washington and National Boulevards, Culver City, ca. 1922

OPPOSITE
Green Mill Gardens advertisement, 1921

GREEN MILL GARDENS

CALIFORNIA'S MOST UNIQUE CAFE

"MORRIE" RAUCH

BILL PAINE

THE GREEN MILL

DINING AND DANCING HALL

RECEPTION LOBBY

"Morrie" Rauch

MORRIS (better known as "Morrie") Rauch is associated with "Bill" Paine as a partner in the proprietorship of the Green Mill Gardens.

Mr. Rauch is one of the best known restaurateurs in Southern California, and in addition to the Green Mill Gardens, owns a chain of popular priced eating houses in Los Angeles and Pasadena.

He is now planning to open an elaborate new Los Angeles cafe to be known as "The Garden of Allah," on Western avenue near Melrose.

Mr. Rauch's success has come through hard work and shrewd investments and he has hosts of friends all over the country who wish him unlimited triumphs at the Green Mill Gardens and all his other culinary enterprises.

The Green Mill Gardens

ALTHOUGH it has been in operation little more than six months, the Green Mill Gardens has become the West's most popular dining and dancing resort.

The unique structure, which resembles an old English Inn, the home-like interior, the general refined atmosphere, and a hundred other details have contributed to its success.

Superb music for dancing is furnished by Snell-Highsmith-Conklin and their famous Green Mill orchestra, with every man a soloist.

Tom Cooney, for twelve years maitre de cuisine at the Van Nuys Hotel, supervises the culinary activities at the Green Mill, and their $2 chicken dinner served nightly is a treat for the palate of the most exacting epicure.

The Green Mill Gardens is popular both for dinner and for after theater parties, and being only twenty-five minutes from Broadway it has added appeal for those who do not want to wander too far away from home.

Special events are staged every Thursday night, including such interesting features as Aviation Balls, Fashion Shows, Song Writers' Contests and the like.

To visit California without seeing the Green Mill Gardens is like going to Rome and not catching a glimpse of the Vatican.

"Bill" Paine

WILLIAM (better known as "Bill") Paine, is associated as a partner with "Morrie" Rauch in the proprietorship of the Green Mill Gardens.

Mr. Paine has been a familiar figure in cafe circles for many years, and is noted for the courtly courteous manner with which he handles the public.

Those who enjoy the Bohemian night life of Southern California have found Mr. Paine on duty as manager of several of the most popular dining and dancing resorts of the West, until in association with Mr. Rauch he decided to "go it on his own" and open the Green Mill Gardens.

On the Washington Highway to Venice

BILL PAINE AND "MORRIE" RAUCH. PROPRIETORS.

ABOVE
Green Mill Gardens, Washington Boulevard at National Boulevard, Culver City, ca. 1922

LEFT
Ham Tree Inn matchcover, ca. 1927

OPPOSITE TOP
Ham Tree, 8641 Washington Boulevard, Culver City, ca. 1927

OPPOSITE BOTTOM
The Burger That Ate L.A., 7624 Melrose Avenue, Los Angeles, 1989

HAMTREE

OPPOSITE
Hawaiian Gardens, Norwalk Boulevard and Carson Street, Artesia, 1930

RIGHT
Hoosegow Café advertisement, 1927

BELOW
Hoosegow Café, 7732 Washington Boulevard, Culver City, ca. 1929

NOW OPEN
ICE CREAM
CANDY
COLD DRINKS
TOBACCO
Hoot! Hoot! I Scream
THE NEW CONFECTIONERY

HOOT HOOT
I SCREAM
1201

PAGES 248–249
Hoot Hoot I Scream, 1201 Valley Boulevard, San Gabriel Valley, 1932

PREVIOUS SPREAD
Iceberg, Los Angeles, ca. 1928

BELOW
Fance Creamery, Oakland, ca. 1931

OPPOSITE
Peterson's Vogue Ice Cream, Los Angeles, 1929

Peterson's
ICE
CREAM
ICE
CREAM

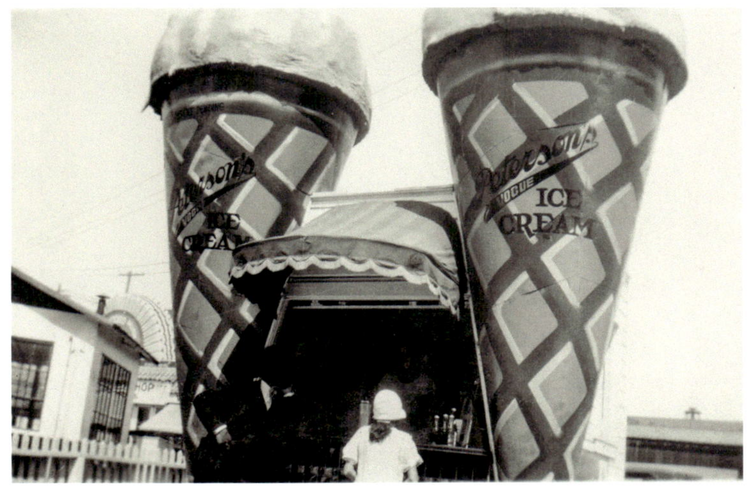

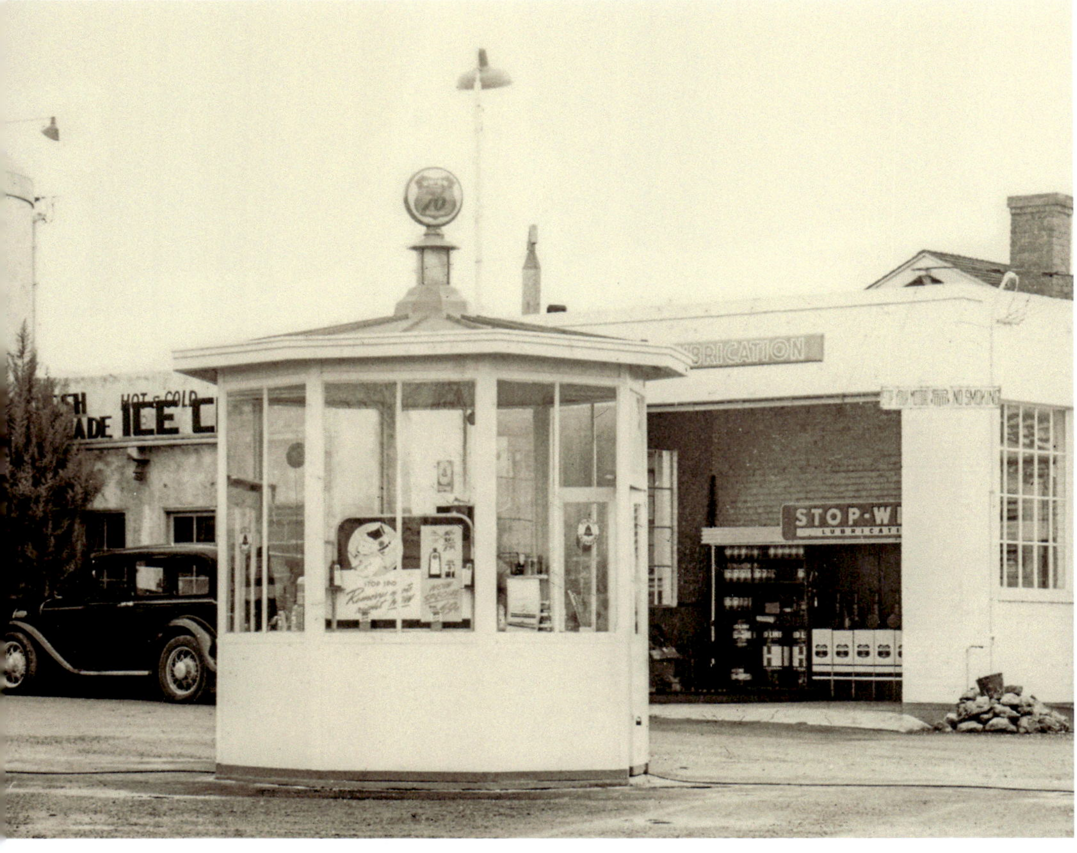
ICE C
LUBRICATION
STOP-WI
NO SMOKING

LEFT
Ice Palace, 3400 Crenshaw Boulevard, Los Angeles, ca. 1929

BELOW
The Igloo, 4302 West Pico Boulevard, Los Angeles, ca. 1928

OPPOSITE
Chapman's Iceberg, Los Angeles, ca. 1933

Chapman's
FANCY ICE CREAMS

IDLE HOUR CAFE

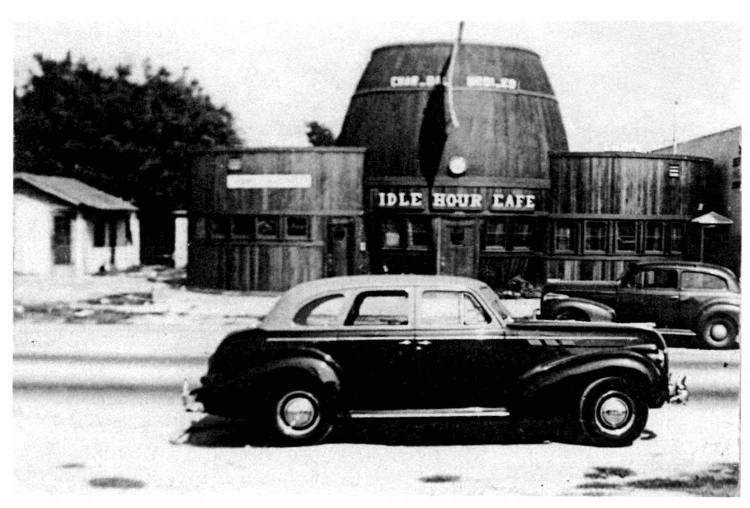

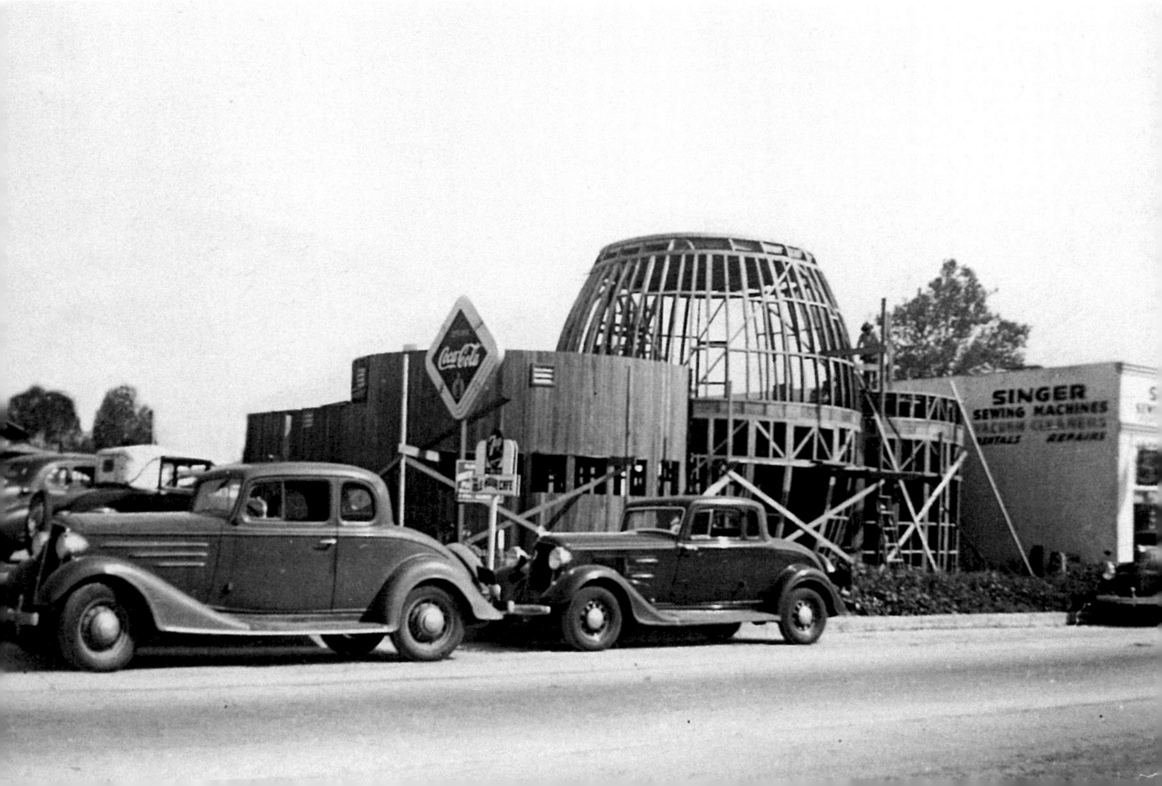
Coca-Cola
SINGER
SEWING MACHINES
REPAIRS

OPPOSITE TOP AND BOTTOM
Idle Hour, 4824 Vineland Avenue, North Hollywood, ca. 1941. Owners: Mr. and Mrs. Michael Connolly

BELOW
Idle Hour, 4824 Vineland Avenue, North Hollywood, 2015

OPPOSITE TOP
Ince Studios, 9336 Washington Boulevard, Culver City, ca. 1928

OPPOSITE BOTTOM
The Indian, Richardson Springs, 1948

THIS PAGE
Jail Café, 4212 Sunset Boulevard, Los Angeles, 1926

Best CHICKEN or STEAK dinner in Town
a whole CHICKEN
French Fries
Corn Pones·Hot Biscuit
Honey·Real Coffee
TOTAL FINE $1.25
EAT·LAUGH·SING·
PLAY GOLF·MUSIC·
DANCING
at Sixth Street
Peppy Entertainment
NO cover charge
5pm to 2:30am·
Sunday 2pm ON
JAILS
LARGE BANQUET CELLS
1207 west 6th St
DRexel 2919
4212 Sunset Blvd
OLympia 2582

OPPOSITE TOP
Jail Café advertisement, 1926

OPPOSITE BOTTOM
Jail Café, 4212 Sunset Boulevard, Los Angeles, 1926

RIGHT
Jesse James Cabin, 11950 Washington Boulevard, Culver City, ca. 1925

BELOW
Jerry's Cabin Café, Culver City, ca. 1926

LEFT
Jumbo Lemon advertisement, 1927

BELOW
Kenyon's Desert Plunge, Park and Adams Avenues, El Centro, 1929. Owner: Fred Kenyon

OPPOSITE
Jumbo Lemon, 1925

DRINK
WITH US
THE JUMBO LEMON
LEMONADE-ORANGEADE

KING'S
TROPICAL INN
CHICKEN DINNERS

KING'S TROPICAL INN
LOS ANGELES, CALIF.
KING'S
TROPICAL INN
CHICKEN DINNERS
MOST FAMOUS CHICKEN DINNERS IN AMERICA
- CORNER WASHINGTON & ADAMS BLVDS. -

OPPOSITE TOP AND MIDDLE
King's Tropical Inn, 5741 West Washington Boulevard, Culver City, ca. 1933. Architect: Frank Dunkin

OPPOSITE BOTTOM
King's Tropical Inn matchbook, ca. 1945

RIGHT
King's Tropical Inn menu, ca. 1929

BELOW
King's Tropical Inn, 5741 West Washington Boulevard, Culver City, ca. 1926

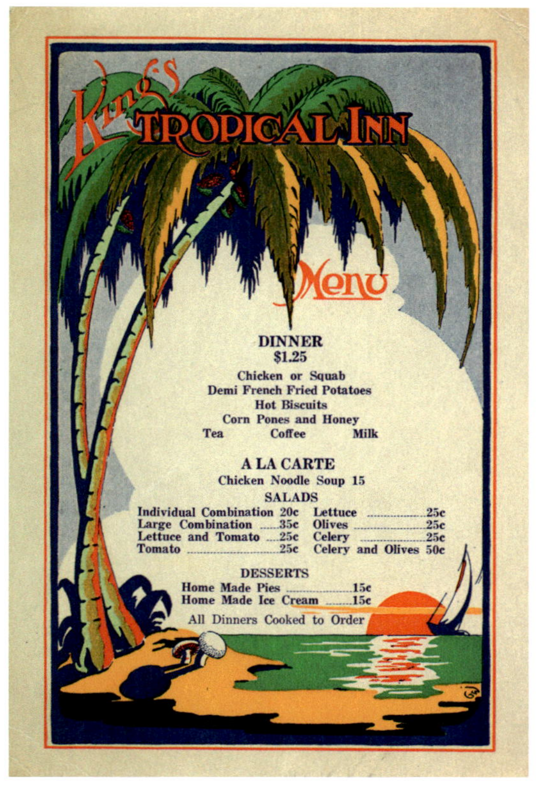

King's
TROPICAL INN
Menu
DINNER
$1.25
Chicken or Squab
Demi French Fried Potatoes
Hot Biscuits
Corn Pones and Honey
Tea Coffee Milk
A LA CARTE
Chicken Noodle Soup 15
SALADS
Individual Combination 20c
Large Combination ......35c
Lettuce and Tomato ......25c
Tomato ......25c
Lettuce ......25c
Olives ......25c
Celery ......25c
Celery and Olives 50c
DESSERTS
Home Made Pies ......15c
Home Made Ice Cream ......15c
All Dinners Cooked to Order

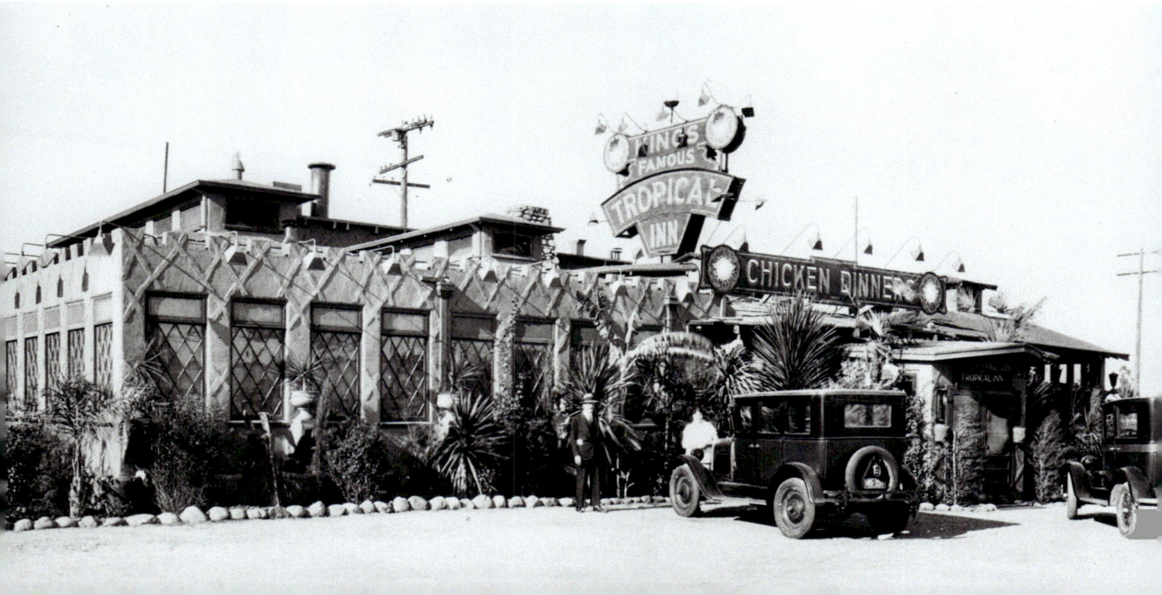
KING'S
FAMOUS
TROPICAL
INN
CHICKEN DINNERS

BELOW
KMTR, 1522 North La Brea Avenue, Los Angeles, 1939

OPPOSITE
Margo Leavin Gallery, 817 North Hilldale Avenue, West Hollywood, 1989. Artists: Claes Oldenburg and Coosje Van Bruggen

ABOVE
The Cone, 402 York Boulevard, Los Angeles, ca. 1932

LEFT
The Feed Rack, 402 York Boulevard, Los Angeles, ca. 1933

OPPOSITE
Shy-Der's Health Juices, 402 York Boulevard, Los Angeles, ca. 1938

FOLLOWING SPREAD
Kone Inn Ice Cream, 402 York Boulevard, Los Angeles, ca. 1931

HEALTH
JUICES
DRINK YOUR Fresh VEGETABLE
SHY-DER'S
100% PURE - UNDILUTED
HEALTH JUICES
DRINK YOUR Fresh VEGETABLE
4854
REVITALIZING
ALKALIZING

KONE INN
ICE CREAM
Our Special MALTED MILK 15
ICE CREAM
PINT QUART
25¢ 45¢

KONE INN
CE CREAM
r Special MALTED MILK
402
ONE INN
in
ice cold mugs
XXX
THIS BUSINESS FRONTAG
QUICK
SERVICE

STAN'S
LIGHTING DISTRIBUTOR
5925
WEST PICO BLVD.
323 935-6626
STAN'S
LIGHTING DISTRIBUTOR
CLEAN & SAFE

OPPOSITE
The Lightbulb, 5925 West Pico Boulevard, Los Angeles, ca. 1995

BELOW
Little Mary's Lighthouse, 6002 Hollywood Boulevard, ca. 1918

LEFT
"He and She" restrooms, Redwood Highway, ca. 1943

BELOW
World's service station, Ukiah, ca. 1944

OPPOSITE TOP
Old Log Cabin, University Avenue, San Diego, 1911

OPPOSITE BOTTOM
My Old Kentucky Home, Huntington Drive, Monrovia, ca. 1933. Owners: Mr. and Mrs. L. M. White

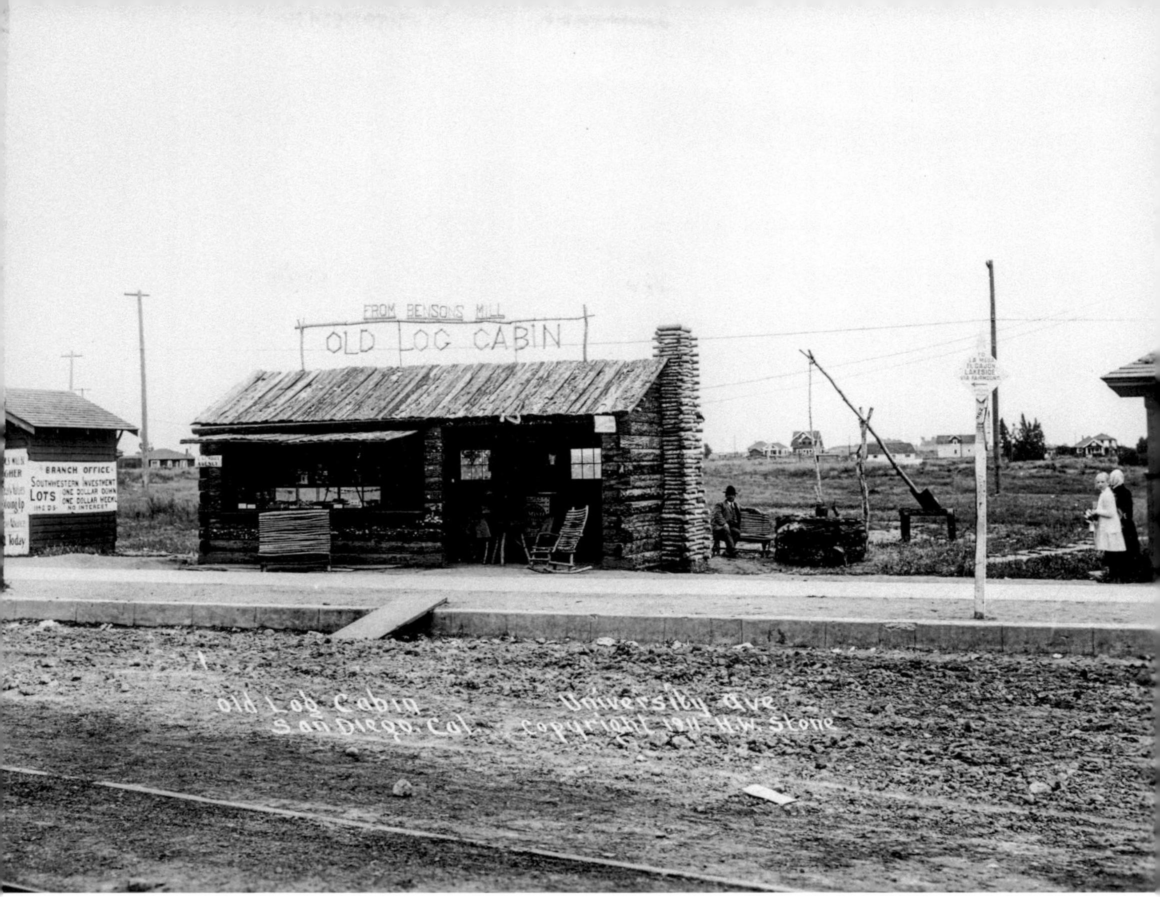

FROM BENSONS MILL
OLD LOG CABIN
BRANCH OFFICE
SOUTHWESTERN INVESTMENT
LOTS
ONE DOLLAR DOWN
ONE DOLLAR WEEKLY
NO INTEREST
Today
Old Log Cabin
San Diego Cal.
University Ave
Copyright 1911 H.W. Stone


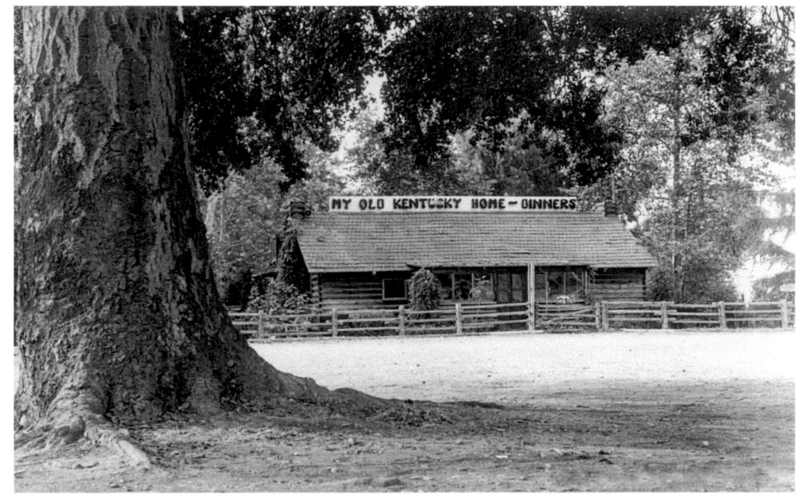

MY OLD KENTUCKY HOME – DINNERS

ABOVE
Mailbox, Los Angeles, 1917

LEFT AND OPPOSITE TOP
Malamute Saloon, ca. 1934

OPPOSITE BOTTOM
Mammy's Shack,
5687 Washington Boulevard,
Los Angeles, ca. 1927

Klondike
orn-Beef
Sandwiches
15
25
25

MAMMY'S SHACK
5687 W. WASHINGTON ST.
LOS ANGELES
CALIF.

ABOVE

Mandarin Market, 1248 Vine Street, Hollywood, ca. 1929. Architect: Henry L. Gogerty

LEFT

Chilitown Café advertisement, 1930

OPPOSITE

Chilitown Café, 1248 Vine Street, Hollywood, ca. 1932

BBER CO.

BELOW
Hollywood Ranch Market, 1248 Vine Street, Hollywood, ca. 1937

OPPOSITE
Mandarin Market, 1248 Vine Street, Hollywood, ca. 1929. Architect: Henry L. Gogerty

The MANDARIN
HERE
MEATS
VEGETABLES
FRUITS
實
10

ELSIE
JANIS

Mayan Theatre, 1040 South Hill Street, Los Angeles, 1927. Architect: Stiles O. Clements

Mayan Theatre, 1040 South Hill Street, Los Angeles, 1927. Architect: Stiles O. Clements

(For 2 People)—$1.50, $2, $2.50 (For 2 People—$2.50, $3, $4)
Mission Village
(For 5 or 6 People)—$5.50 or $6.00
"Motor Court"
(For 2 People)—$1.50, $2, $2.50 (For 2 People—$2.50, $3, $4)
Mission Village
Famous Movie Stars — Visit Village —
Among the numerous movie stars who consider the Village an unusual place of charm are: Joan Blondell, Bette Davis, Wallace Beery, Joan Crawford, Mickey Rooney, Roscoe Ates, Henry Fonda, Jack LaRue, Commodore J. Steuart-Blackton, George Raft. Many others have paid the Village a fellowship visit.
Be sure to see
Our Indian Theatre
Wishing Well - Mystic Spirit Den - 12,000 Lucky Horseshoes and Free Information Room
— Movie Homes — Reliable Guides
To Movie Star Homes Studios - Beaches - and all points of interest in city or Southern California
Where Worth-while People Meet
"The Place Where You Have Good Luck"
Where You Will Feel at Home
Most Unique Tourist Court in America.
Mission Village
5675 W. Washington Blvd Los Angeles, California
$100,000.00 Enterprise—Midway Between Downtwon and the Beaches. Catering to the Better Type Traveling Public
Founded 1929
Phone WHitney 2652
Erected and Owned by Robert E. Callahan, Author and Producer of the End of the Trail at the World's Fair.
Colorful Mission and — Indian Setting —
Originally conceived as an Indian Art Center—later developed as Mission Bungalows — Indian Pueblos — Tepee Homes and esta" Hall for the comfort of westbound travelers. The village was designed, erected and is still owned and operated by the founder and creator.
Unique Enterprise Established 10 Years No Other Like It
Each year our business has increased—each year new guests arrive who were sent here by former guests, proving that economy, courtesy, and a friendly spirit pay in spreading the news about Mission Village.
5 Acre Area Close In
Cozy - Quiet - Restful - Distinctive - Fine Beds
Tile Showers Refrigeration - Day and Night
Near Market - School - Church - Club
Near the Picture Studios
—Only 10 to 15— — minutes to — Beaches, Fishing,- — Race Track, — Baseball, Skating- —Golf, Bowling— —or Playgrounds—
Good-Luck "Teepees"—Mission Village
The Creator and Owner of Mission Village
Robert E. Callahan
Author of 9 novels—21 serials and over 1000 radio programs Originator of Death Valley Days broadcast. His latest novel – "Wife Wanted"—thrilling serial success—is now in book form and already transcribed into radio shows.
Private Trailer Garden
Tile Showers - Rolled Gravel - Clean Grounds
Well Lighted - Fiesta Hall - Ping Pong - Billiards
$3.50 or $4.00 Per Week - $12 - $14 Per Month
Unusual and Fascinating
- Entire Grounds - - Surrounded by - 9-ft. Mission Wall. —No Tents—No— —Camping, and— — No Solicitors — — Allowed. —
Private Trailers—Mission Village
5675-77 West Washington Boulevard
Los Angeles Phone WHitney 2652
5675-77 West Washington Boulevard
Los Angeles Phone WHitney 2652
5675-77 West Washington Boulevard
Los Angeles Phone WHitney 2652

OPPOSITE TOP

Merlin Hat, Walt Disney Animation Studios, 2100 West Riverside Drive, Burbank, 1996. Architect: Robert A. M. Stern

OPPOSITE BOTTOM

Mission Village brochure, ca. 1938

RIGHT

Mission Village advertisement, ca. 1938

BELOW

Mission Village, 5600 West Washington Boulevard, Los Angeles, ca. 1939

ABOVE AND LEFT
Mission Village, 5600 West Washington Boulevard, Los Angeles, ca. 1939

OPPOSITE
Ramona Village, 5600 West Washington Boulevard, Los Angeles, 1929

A $50,000.00 Benefit Entertainment—Don't Miss It!
Buffalo Barbecue! Rodeo! Sham Battle!
Fancy Riders! Trick Ropers! Stampede!
COWBOYS! INDIANS!
March 8-9-10
Fri-Sat-Sun
Gates Open 7:30 P. M.
Matinee 2 P. M. Sat-Sun
Benefit Affair
Any Profit Derived will be Used Toward Further Developing this Historical and Educational Enterprise
HISTORIC ABORIGINAL EDUCATIONAL ETHNOLOGICAL INDUSTRIAL EXHIBITION
COL. F. T. CUMMINS
COL. FRED CUMMINS, (Chief La-Ko-Ta) Director-General
Stampede Rodeo Alive With Color and
FREE BUFFALO BARBECUE
Admission $1.00 (One Section Seats 50c Extra, None Higher) Children 50c
Ramona Village Grounds
(Four acre area)
5600 block West Washington
LOS ANGELES
March 8 · 9 · 10
EXECUTIVE COMMITTEE—D. W. Pontius, C. C. C. Tatum, Sheriff William I. Traeger, F. P. Newport, L. E. Behymer, Frank Tenney Johnson, Orra Monnette, Rex B. Goodcell, A. Carman Smith, Dr. Walter F. Dexter, Robert E. Callahan, Charles P. McFaul, Eugene Biscailuz, Under Sheriff; Charles Wakefield Cadman, James Davis, Chief of Police; John Boos, Maurice DeMond, J. B. Duffy, Johnny S. Arrington, Walter Danburg, Harry Hammond Beall. CULVER CITY COMMITTEE—A. N. Bacon, John King, Wm. Shea, Foster Curry, Reve Houck. GROUND COMMITTEE—Nick Harris, Ford Jack, Al Copeland, Snowy Baker, George W. Atterbery Sam Garrett, Ranger Miller, Hosea Steelman, Capt. S. L. Hoffman, Thomas Getz.
Live Wild Buffalos Now on the Grounds. Your Children Should See Them

ABOVE

Residence of Aimee Semple McPherson and David Hutton, Lake Elsinore, ca. 1930

LEFT

El Miradero, Glendale, ca. 1921. Architect: Nathaniel Dryden. Owner: Leslie C. Brand

RIGHT
Washington Brake Service advertisement, ca. 1960

BELOW
Persian Market, 12137 Washington Place, Los Angeles, 1929. Architect: George M. Thomas

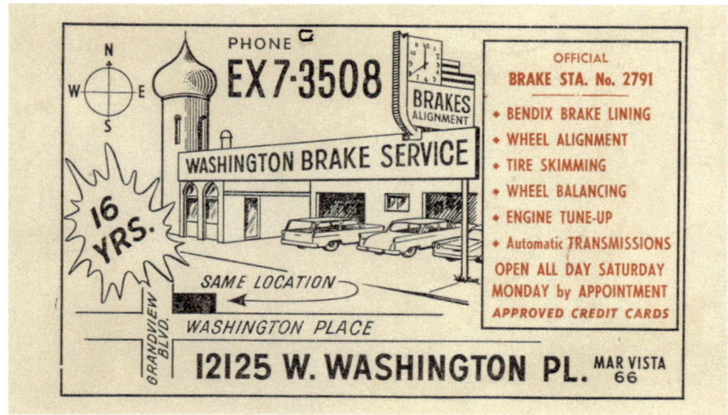

LEFT

Angeles Abbey, 1515 East Compton Boulevard, Compton, ca. 1934

BELOW

Bundy and Albright Real Estate, 15410 Ventura Boulevard, Sherman Oaks, ca. 1934

TOP
Pacific Southwest Exposition, Long Beach, 1928

BOTTOM
Moorish-themed apartments, Los Angeles, ca. 1927

BELOW
Sniff's Date Garden,
Highway 111, Indio, ca. 1949

OPPOSITE
Self-Realization Fellcwship,
4860 Sunset Boulevard,
Los Angeles, ca. 1952

MUSHROOMBURGERS

LEFT
Motel Inn, ca. 1942

BELOW
Motel Inn, 2223 Monterey Street, San Luis Obispo, ca. 1925. Architect: Arthur Heineman

OPPOSITE
Motel Inn brochure, ca. 1926

COFFEE SHOP

Complete Hotel Service in Bungalows
THIS is the Mo-tel Inn, on the Coast Highway at the north end of San Luis Obispo. Quiet—comfortable—moderate.
(FIREPROOF)

Mother Goose Pantry, 1959 East Colorado Boulevard, Pasadena, ca. 1929

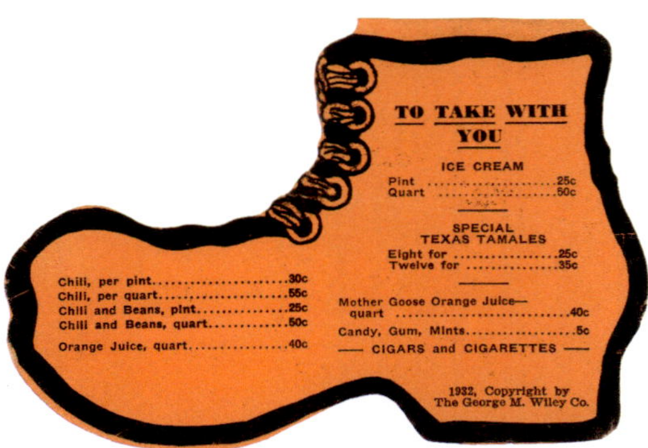

THIS PAGE
Mother Goose Pantry menu, ca. 1929

OPPOSITE TOP
Mother Goose Pantry, 1959 East Colorado Boulevard, Pasadena, ca. 1929

OPPOSITE BOTTOM
Mother Goose Pantry and The Big Shoe matchcovers, ca. 1930

MOTHER
GOOSE
PANTRY
1959 E. COLORADO ST.
PASADENA, CALIF.

The
BIG SHOE
1959 E. COLORADO

LEFT
Mt. Baldy Inn, 9608 Whittier Boulevard, Pico Rivera, ca. 1976

BELOW
The Mountains, Garfield and Whittier Boulevards, Montebello, ca. 1928

OPPOSITE TOP
Mt. Baldy Inn, 9608 Whittier Boulevard, Pico Rivera, 1927

OPPOSITE BOTTOM
Mt. Baldy Frozen Orange Juice Stand, 9608 Whittier Boulevard, Pico Rivera, ca. 1928. Owners: Gar and Lily McOmber

BARBECUE

WHITTIER BOULEVARD
PUT
Eastside
INSIDE
PERFECT BREW

PREVIOUS SPREAD
Mushrooms Café, 3500 West Olive Avenue, Burbank, ca. 1927

OPPOSITE
Oil Can, Whittier Boulevard, East Los Angeles, ca. 1935

RIGHT
The Oil Well service station, ca. 1925

BELOW
Dave Kirschner Richfield station, 176 South Alvarado Street, Los Angeles, ca. 1932

SERVICE
SERVICE

OPPOSITE
Oil Derrick, ca. 1921

ABOVE
Orange Blossom, Valley Boulevard between El Monte and La Puente, ca. 1923. Owners: Mr. and Mrs. Ray Hutchins

RIGHT
Orange Blossom Inn matchcover, ca. 1926

Light Lunches at Counter
ORANGE BLOSSOM INN
VALLEY BOULEVARD
MIDWAY
BETWEEN EL MONTE & PUENTE

LEFT AND OPPOSITE BOTTOM
Orange Inn, 2958 Foothill Boulevard, Pasadena, ca. 1924

BELOW
Orange Inn, 2958 Foothill Boulevard, Pasadena, 1927

OPPOSITE TOP
Orange Blossom Inn, La Puente, ca. 1926

The ORANGE BLOSSOM
WHOLESALE & RETAIL

Every thing In Oranges,
2958. Foothill Blvd, Pasadena Calif.

LEFT
Petaluma Chicken, ca. 1931

BELOW
Petaluma Chicken, ca. 1927

OPPOSITE TOP
Beatrice Hatchery advertising sign, Petaluma, ca. 1947

OPPOSITE BOTTOM
Petaluma Egg Basket, ca. 1927

BEATRICE
HATCHERY

COLD STORAGE CO
PETALUMA
THE WORLD'S EGG BASKET
PRODUCES ANNUALLY
45,000,000 DOZEN EGGS
Petaluma,
California

LEFT
Pirate's Cove, 4949 Santa Monica Avenue, San Diego, 2009

BELOW
Pharoah's Lost Kingdom, 1100 California Street, Redlands, 1996

OPPOSITE
Pickle Bill's Bar-B-Q, 2714 Pico Boulevard, Santa Monica, 1971. Owners: Harvey and Florence Davenport

PICKLE
BILL'S
BAR-B-Q
PICKLE BILLS
FRENCH DIPPE
ST
DIFFERENT
FOUNTA
NO PARKING 3-5 A.M.
REAL ESTATE
AUTOMOTIV
OPEN
6 Pak

PREVIOUS SPREAD
Pig Café, La Brea and Rosewood Avenues, Los Angeles, ca. 1934

ABOVE
Plantation Cafe, 7600 West Washington Boulevard, Los Angeles, ca. 1923

LEFT
Plantation Club menu, 1922

OPPOSITE
Roscoe Arbuckle's Plantation Café menu, 1928

"WHERE THE STARS COME OUT"
Roscoe Arbuckle's PLANTATION

Roscoe Arbuckle's
PLANTATION CAFE
CULVER CITY
CALIFORNIA
DINNER MENU
$2.00 PER PERSON
SEAFOOD OR FRUIT COCKTAIL
CANAPE OF ANCHOVIES
CELERY VICTOR WITH ANCHOVIES
BABY ARTICHOKE, RICHELIEU
CRISP CELERY
RIPE COLOSSAL OLIVE
SOUPS
CONSOMME
SOUP DU JOUR
CHICKEN BROTH
CHOICE
CORN FED CHICKEN PLANTATION, OR A SEC
BROOK TROUT SAUTE, BROWN BUTTER
BROILED SQUAB WITH BACON
FROG LEG SAUTE, FATTY ARBUCKLE SPECIAL
TENDERLOIN OF BEEF GOULASH, A LA DEUTCH
VIRGINIA HAM STEAK. LOUISIANA
LAMB CHOPS, MIXED GRILL
N. Y. CUT SIRLOIN OR FILET MIGNON
HALF BROILED LOBSTER, FRENCH FRIED
VEGETABLE
POTATOES
SALAD DU SASON
CHOICE
ASSORTED ICE CREAM SUNDAES
PETIT FOURS
HOMEMADE PIES
DEMI TASSE

OPPOSITE
Roscoe Arbuckle's Plantation Café menu, 1928

RIGHT
The Plantation advertisement, 1922

FAR RIGHT
Roscoe Arbuckle's Plantation Café advertisement, 1929

BELOW
Roscoe Arbuckle's Plantation Café, 7600 West Washington Boulevard, Los Angeles, ca. 1928

ABOVE AND OPPOSITE TOP
Pumpkin Palace, 3611 Magnolia Boulevard, Burbank, ca. 1927

LEFT
Pumpkin Inn, 3611 Magnolia Boulevard, Burbank, 1927

OPPOSITE BOTTOM
Valley Gospel Center, 3611 Magnolia Boulevard, Burbank, ca. 1935

MENU
Special
Steak Dinners
PLEASE
KEEP OUT

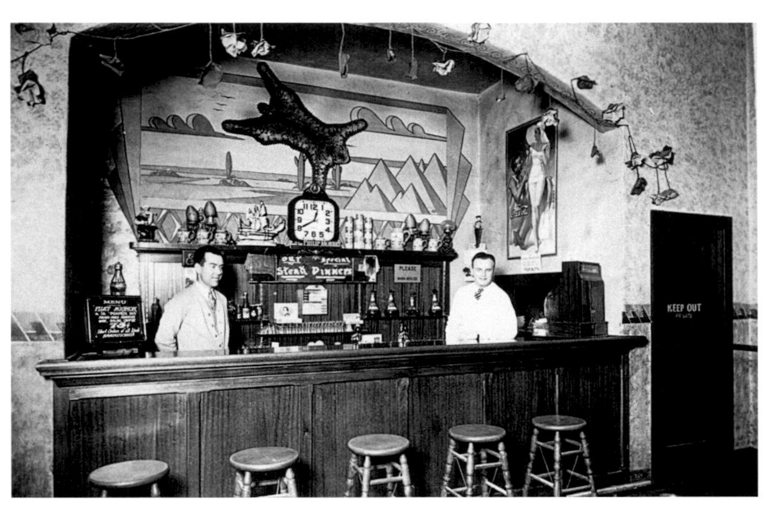

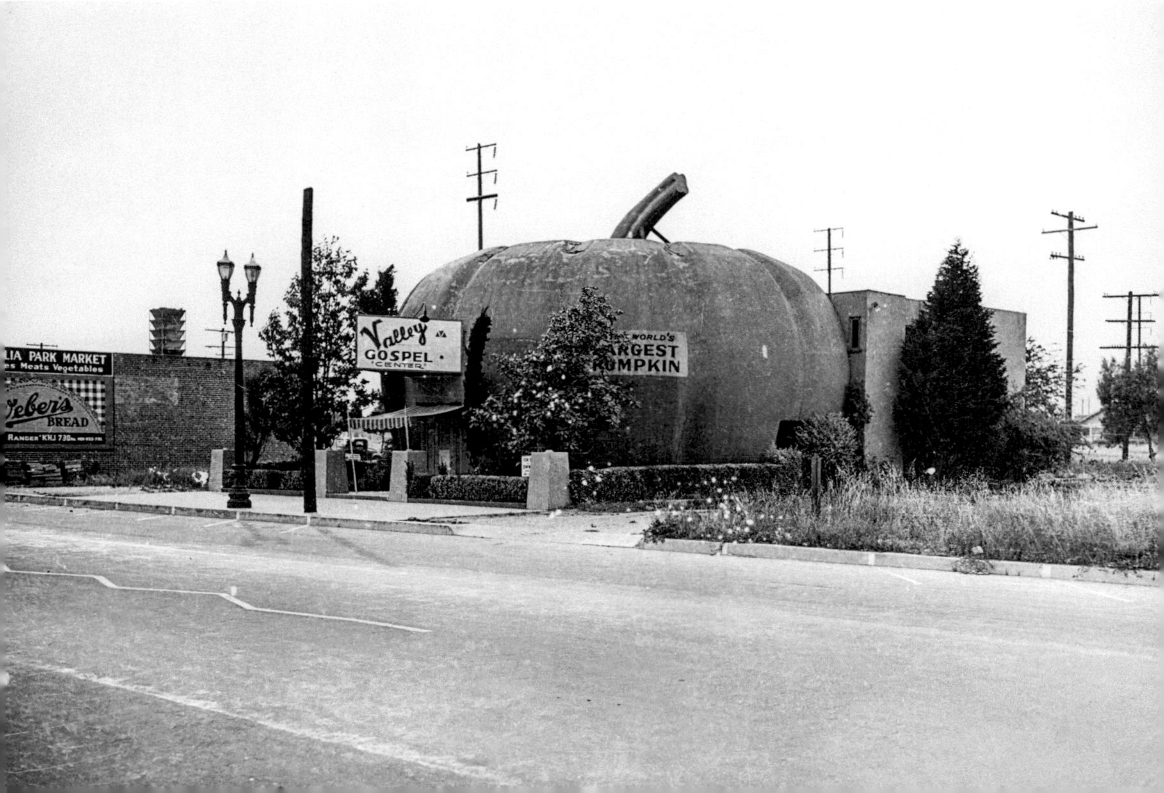
LIA PARK MARKET
Meats Vegetables
BREAD
Valley
GOSPEL
"CENTER"
WORLD'S
ARGEST
UMPKIN

PREVIOUS SPREAD
Pup Café, 12732 West Washington Boulevard, Culver City, 1929

LEFT
Pup Café, 12732 West Washington Boulevard, Culver City, ca. 1940

BELOW
Pyramid Cube University, South Atlantic Boulevard and West Mission Street, Alhambra, 1931. Owner: Frank E. Ormsby

OPPOSITE
Rabbit, South Figueroa Street, Los Angeles, ca. 1928

ABOVE
Redwood restaurant, Venice, 1918

OPPOSITE TOP
Rice Bowl, 909 16th Street, Merced, 1998

OPPOSITE BOTTOM
RKO Studios, Gower Street at Melrose Avenue, Los Angeles, 1949

PEPSI
RICE BOWL
RICE
BOWL
OPEN

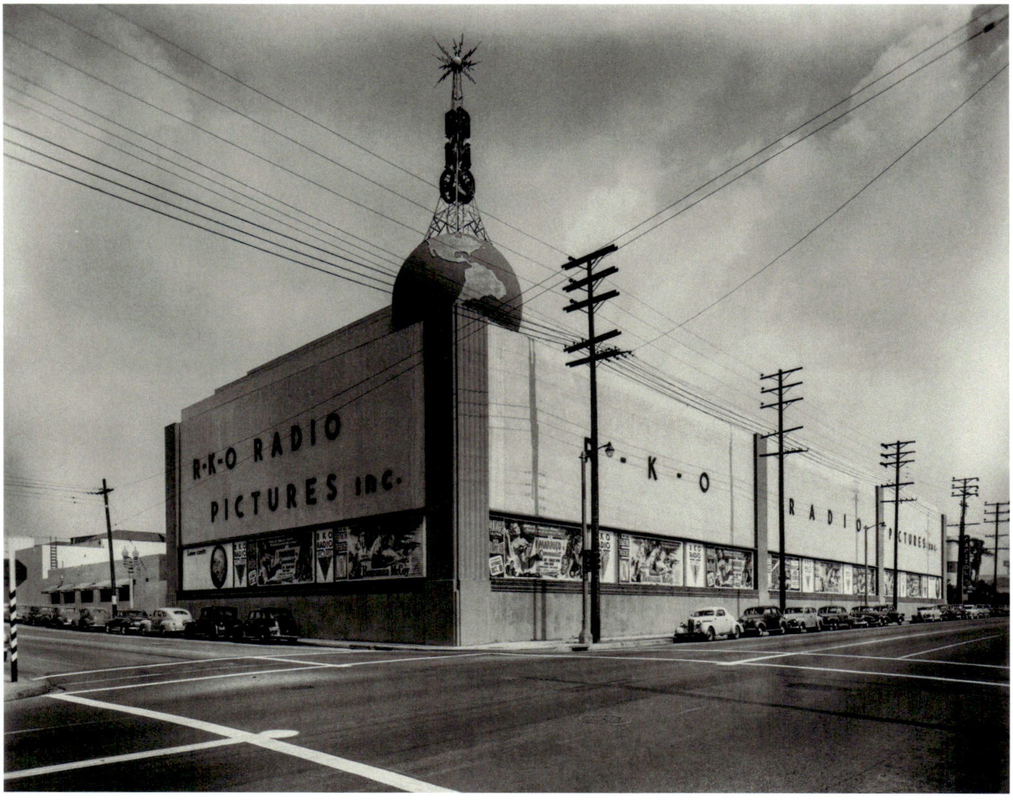

BELOW
Al's Service, ca. 1937

OPPOSITE
The Apple House, ca. 1932

NEHI
TAKE A GOOD LOOK
LUNCH
GOOD SANDWICHES
OFFICIAL
HOUSE
VEGATABLES
& RETAIL
CIDER
LET'S EAT
BREAD
FROZEN
ORANGE-JUICE
Free
PAGEANT
INFORMATION
FRESH
VEGETABLES

ROUND HOUSE
CAFE
STOP
LOOK
EAT
ROUND HOUSE

OPPOSITE
Round House Café, 250 North Virgil Avenue, Los Angeles, 1927

RIGHT
Samson Tires advertisement, ca. 1929

BELOW
Samson Tires, 5675 Telegraph Road, City of Commerce, ca. 1930. Architect: Morgan, Walls, and Clements. Owner: Adolph Schleicher

Samson Tires,
5675 Telegraph Road,
City of Commerce, ca. 1939.
Owner: Adolph Schleicher

LEFT
Sanderson Hosiery opening, 11711 Olympic Boulevard, Los Angeles, 1949

BELOW
Sanderson Hosiery matchcover, 1949

OPPOSITE
Sanderson Hosiery, 11711 Olympic Boulevard, Los Angeles, ca. 1948. Owner: A. A. Sanderson

NYLONS

AND
The DATE SHOP
RE IS WHERE YOU GET SANTA'S FAMOUS DATE SHAKES
SANDWICHES
US RURAL
POST OFFICE

OPPOSITE
Santa Claus Juice Bar,
U.S. 101, Carpinteria, ca. 1954

ABOVE
Snowman Café,
U.S. 101, Carpinteria, ca. 1954

SANTA CLAUS
JUICE BAR
DATE
CANDY DATES HONEY
OLIVES, CIGARETTES
DOLLS NOVELTIES
GIFT SHOP
JUICE BAR
WE SHIP FROM Santa Claus
ALL OVER THE WORLD
Ice Cre
WELCOME TO
SANTA CLAUS CALIF.
Largest SANTA CLAUS in the U.S.A.
Santa Claus, Calif.
via Carpinteria, Calif

OPPOSITE TOP
Santa Claus Juice Bar, U.S. 101, Carpinteria, ca. 1954

OPPOSITE BOTTOM
Santa's Kitchen, U.S. 101, Carpinteria, ca. 1958

ABOVE
Self-Realization Fellowship, 4860 Sunset Boulevard, Los Angeles, 1951

RIGHT
Shell Oil exhibit, California Pacific International Exposition, San Diego, 1935

OPPOSITE
Ship Café, Venice Pier, ca. 1908

RIGHT
Ship Café menu, ca. 1925

BELOW
Ship Café, Venice Pier, ca. 1923

# The Joy Ship of the World

Capt. J. M. Covington, Proprietor

Covington Ship Cafe

THE traditions of the "Cabrillo," Venice, will live as long as the surging waves of the Pacific, because the Covington Ship Cafe—The Joy Ship of the World—is a most faithful reproduction of the craft in which the famous Spanish explorer Juan Rodriguez Cabrillo sailed into Santa Monica Bay on October 9, 1542.

You are hailed aboard the S.S. Cabrillo—The Joy Ship of the World—by the cheery voice of Capt. Covington. Leaving the gangway of this $100,000 ship the first impression created is that you are standing on the deck of an Armada flagship far out at sea. However, landlubbers need have no fear, as The Joy Ship of the World is safely docked above the rolling waves of the Pacific Ocean. She is nearly 300 feet from stem to stern, with a beam of 80 feet, and a moulded depth of 35 feet. From the bow a wonderful panorama of the beautiful Bay of Santa Monica can be seen in all its grandeur, with mountains rising in all their majesty, in terrace after terrace, until they are lost in the soft haze of the high Sierras, 5000 feet above sea level, rivaling the famous Bay of Naples, Italy.

Looking aft, the ship's masts tower some hundred feet above her stately deck. The lookout or "crow's nest" is equipped with a powerful searchlight which at night throws its welcome rays well toward Los Angeles, inviting those who desire to reach The Joy Ship of the World by way of Washington or Pico boulevards, the shortest routes from the business and residential sections of the city.

Day or night the main dining saloon of The Joy Ship of the World offers a vivid picture of cosmopolitan life. Constructed as it is on most imposing lines, it is a most fitting background for the fashionably gowned women and smart looking men who frequent it.

Spacious decks aft and forward accommodate dinner parties, affording quiet seclusion, such as would be enjoyed aboard private yachts. The main saloon amidships will comfortably seat 700 diners, permitting easy access and an unobstructed view of the justly famous dancing floor which is the joy of merry throngs in rhythmic motion to the superb music of the Ship's trained musicians. Music on The Joy Ship of the World is not the usual class of cafe music. The musicians are as well versed in symphony music as they are in the lighter forms of composition.

The Ship's galley is equipped with the latest culinary devices and replete with the most modern ideals of sanitation. A cordial invitation is extended to visit it at all times. It is the equal of any ship's galley to be found on any ocean greyhound.

While the selection of food for service on The Joy Ship of the World is of the highest quality, the charges are only in proportion to their excellence. The Covington Ship Cafe is "popular" rather than "exclusive." Capt. J. M. Covington, proprietor, spares neither trouble nor expense to give the epicure of the present age the same splendid service that the epicurean Spaniards of Cabrillo's time demanded. Each section of The Joy Ship of the World in point of service is similar in every respect to that found on an Atlantic liner. Cordiality and direct contact with all officers of the Covington Ship Cafe give a feeling of pleasure and satisfaction. Obtrusive service is not permitted on the Ship.

The main dining saloon of The Joy Ship of the World is decorated in two-tone Tiffany, a combination that mokes for a stately beauty. Lighting is excellent and artistic. The subdued effect creates an atmosphere all its own and makes The Covington Ship Cafe the recognized rendezvous of the best elements of society.

Parking reservations are provided on the Ship's pier for cars and reservation for special dinner parties can be made by phoning Santa Monica 61069.

This is the simple tale of "Ye Good Ship Cabrillo"—Captain Covington's Ship Cafe—better known perhaps as The Joy Ship of the World, firmly moored at the new Venice pier on Santa Monica Bay.

Main Dining Saloon

Aft Dining Saloon

The Captain's Table

Forward Dining Saloon

At the Ship's Gangway

OPPOSITE
Ship Café article, 1921
RIGHT
Ship Café advertisement, 1922
BELOW
Ship Café postcard, ca. 1908

BELOW
Deschwanden's Shoe Repair, 931 Chester Avenue, Bakersfield, ca. 1985. Owner: Chester Deschwanden

OPPOSITE TOP
Showboat, 3242 Cahuenga Boulevard, Los Angeles, 1980

OPPOSITE BOTTOM
Shutter Shack, 15336 Goldenwest Street, Westminster, ca. 1980. Designer: Susan Del Monte

B.B.Q. RIBS
HOT DOGS
CHEESE BURGER
B.B.Q. HAM
SHOWBOAT
BROASTED CHICKEN
Coca-Cola
SHOWBOAT
ALI'S BROASTED CHICKEN
Coca-Cola
OPEN

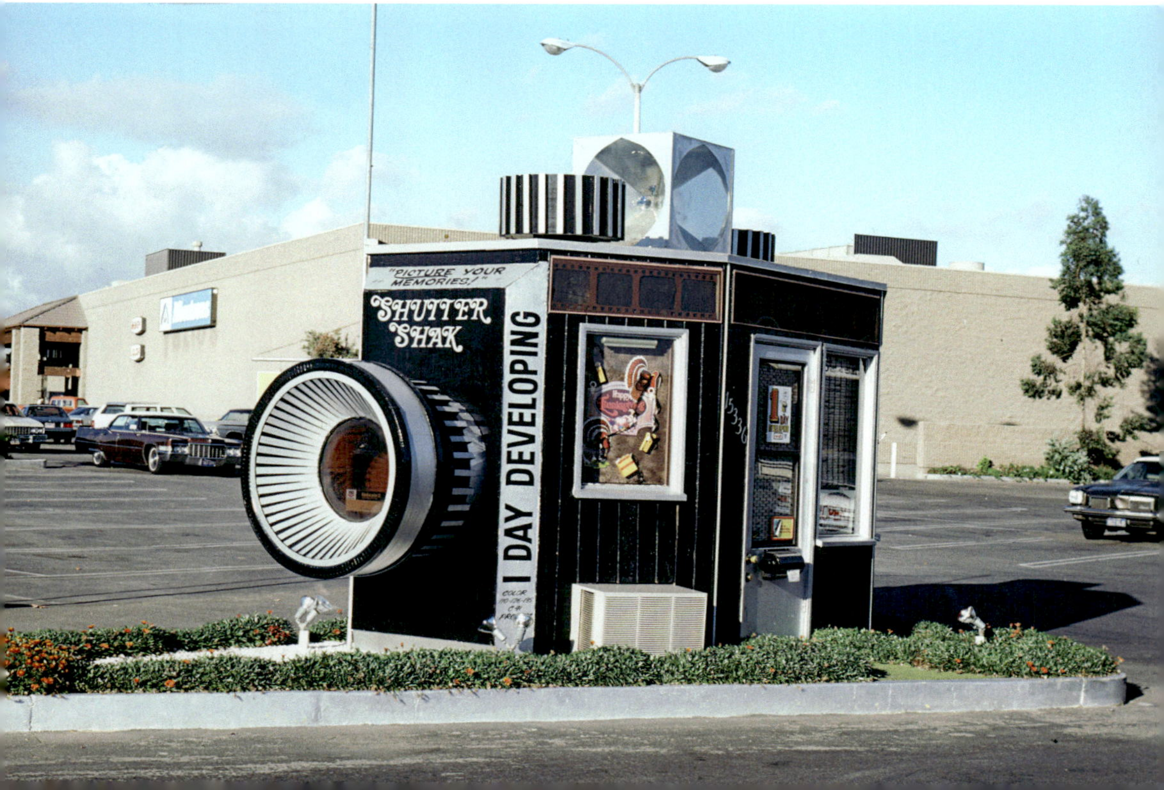

OPPOSITE TOP
Sniff's Date Garden, California State Highway 111, Indio, ca. 1926

OPPOSITE BOTTOM
Soboba Theatre, Main Street, San Jacinto, ca. 1927. Architect: Frederic Johnston. Owners: Oscar Hoffman and Leslie Reynolds

ABOVE
Shrine Auditorium, 665 West Jefferson Boulevard, Los Angeles, ca. 1926

BELOW
Shrine Auditorium, 665 West Jefferson Boulevard, Los Angeles, ca. 1915

SNIFF'S
The SNIFFS Invite You to Visit their UNUSUAL GARDENS

SAN JACINTO VALLEY
CHAMBER OF COMMERCE
PHIL HARRIS CHARLIE RUGGLES
MELODY CRUISE
SOBOBA INDIAN SHOP
Soboba theatre San Jacinto Calif.

OPPOSITE AND BELOW
Soboba Hot Springs,
San Jacinto, ca. 1924

RIGHT
Soboba Hot Springs
stationery detail, ca. 1924

BELOW
Sphinx Realty, 537 North Fairfax Avenue, Los Angeles, ca. 1940

OPPOSITE
Sphinx Realty, 537 North Fairfax Avenue, Los Angeles, 1926

LET US
SELL IT
OPEN
CORNER
NEAR HERE
$ 2800

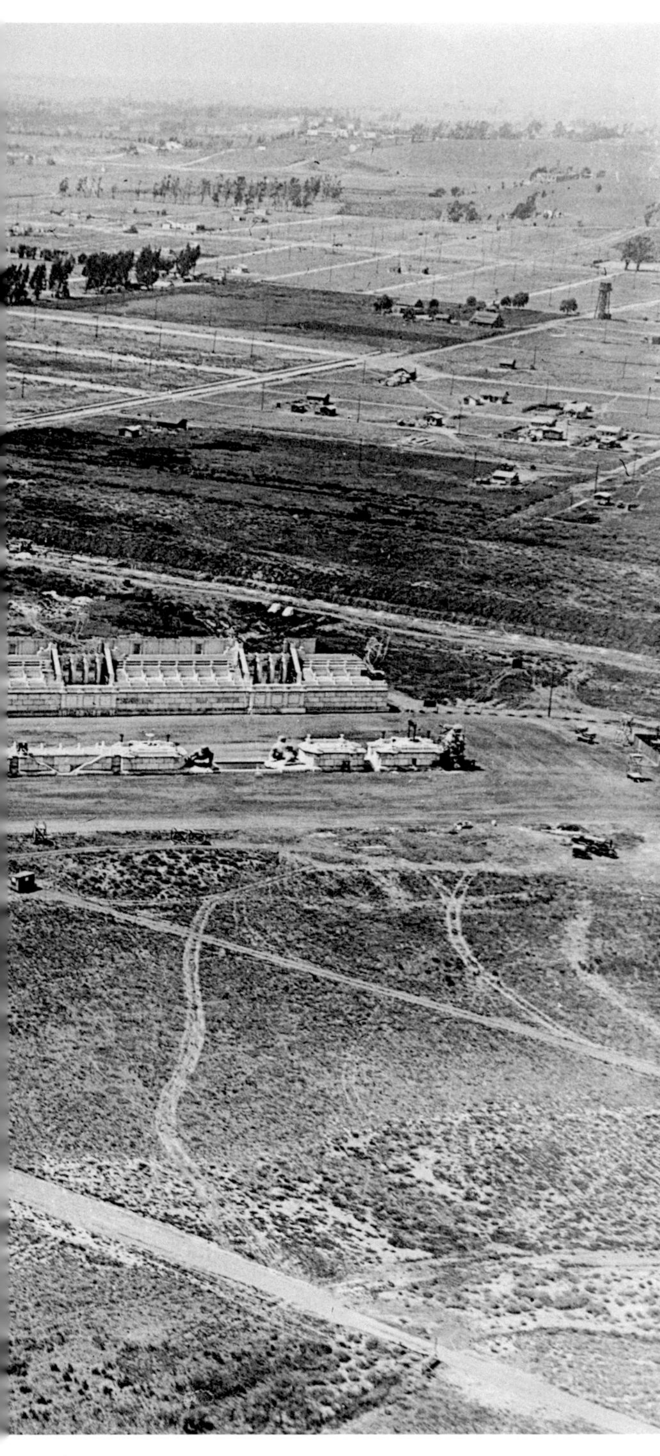

*Ben Hur* set, La Cienega and Venice Boulevards, Los Angeles, 1925

OPPOSITE TOP AND BOTTOM
Studio backlots, Hollywood, ca. 1926

ABOVE
RKO-Pathé Studios backlot, Culver City, 1929

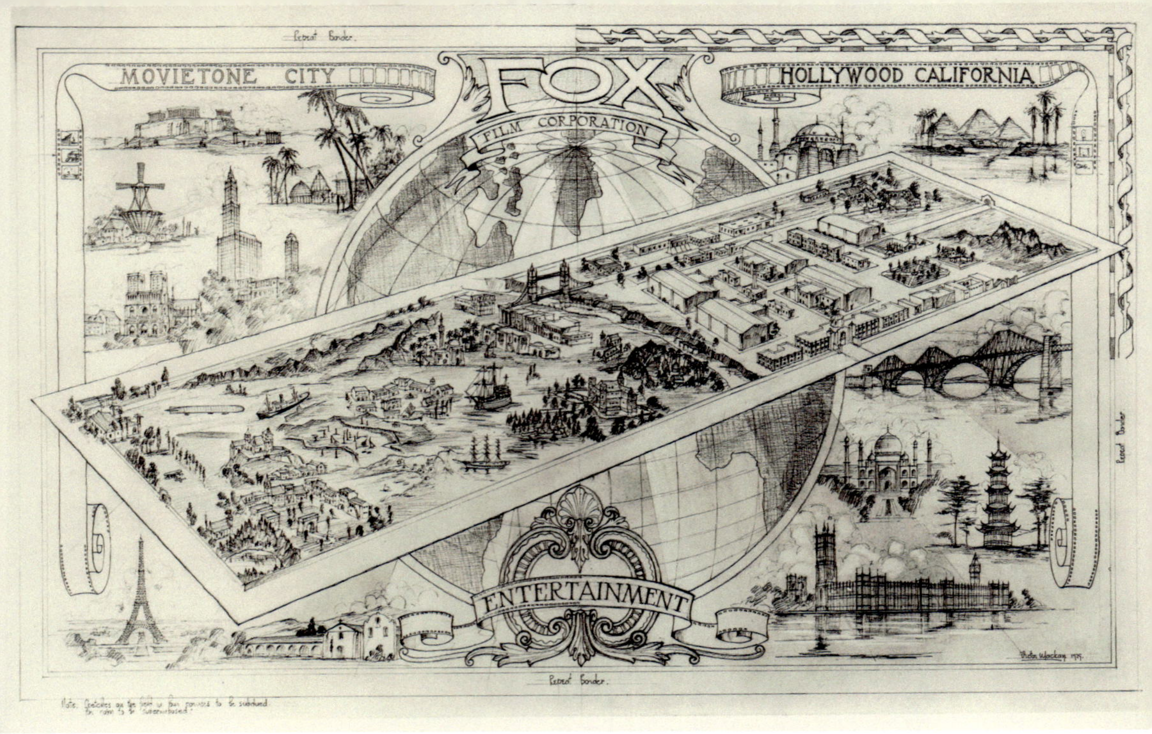


ABOVE
Fox Movietone Studio map, ca. 1929

OPPOSITE TOP
Selig Polyscope Company, East Los Angeles, ca. 1919

OPPOSITE BOTTOM
*Intolerance* set, Sunset Boulevard at Hillhurst Avenue, Los Angeles, 1918

FOLLOWING SPREAD
Studio backlots, Universal City, ca. 1916

MAIN ENTRANCE

CHILI
DOGS
35¢
TASTY
HOT PUPS
YOU'LL LIKE EM
Coca-Cola
HOT DO
TELEPHONE
TELEPHONE
KRAUT
PUP
35¢

PUBLIC
TELEPHONE
TAIL
O' the
PUP
311 NO LA CIENEGA

TAIL o'the PUP

PREVIOUS SPREAD
Tail o' the Pup, 311 North La Cienega Boulevard, Los Angeles, ca. 1959

OPPOSITE TOP
Tail o' the Pup, 311 North La Cienega Boulevard, Los Angeles, ca. 1947

OPPOSITE BOTTOM
Tail o' the Pup, 329 San Vicente Boulevard, Los Angeles, ca. 2000

THIS PAGE
Tail o' the Pup reopening, 8512 Santa Monica Boulevard, Los Angeles, 2022

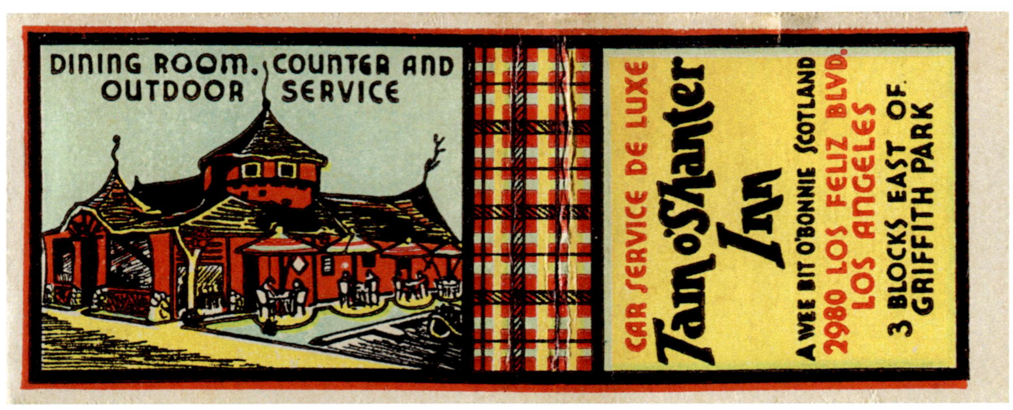

DINING ROOM. COUNTER AND
OUTDOOR SERVICE
CAR SERVICE DE LUXE
Tam O'Shanter Inn
A WEE BIT O'BONNIE SCOTLAND
2980 LOS FELIZ BLVD.
LOS ANGELES
3 BLOCKS EAST OF
GRIFFITH PARK

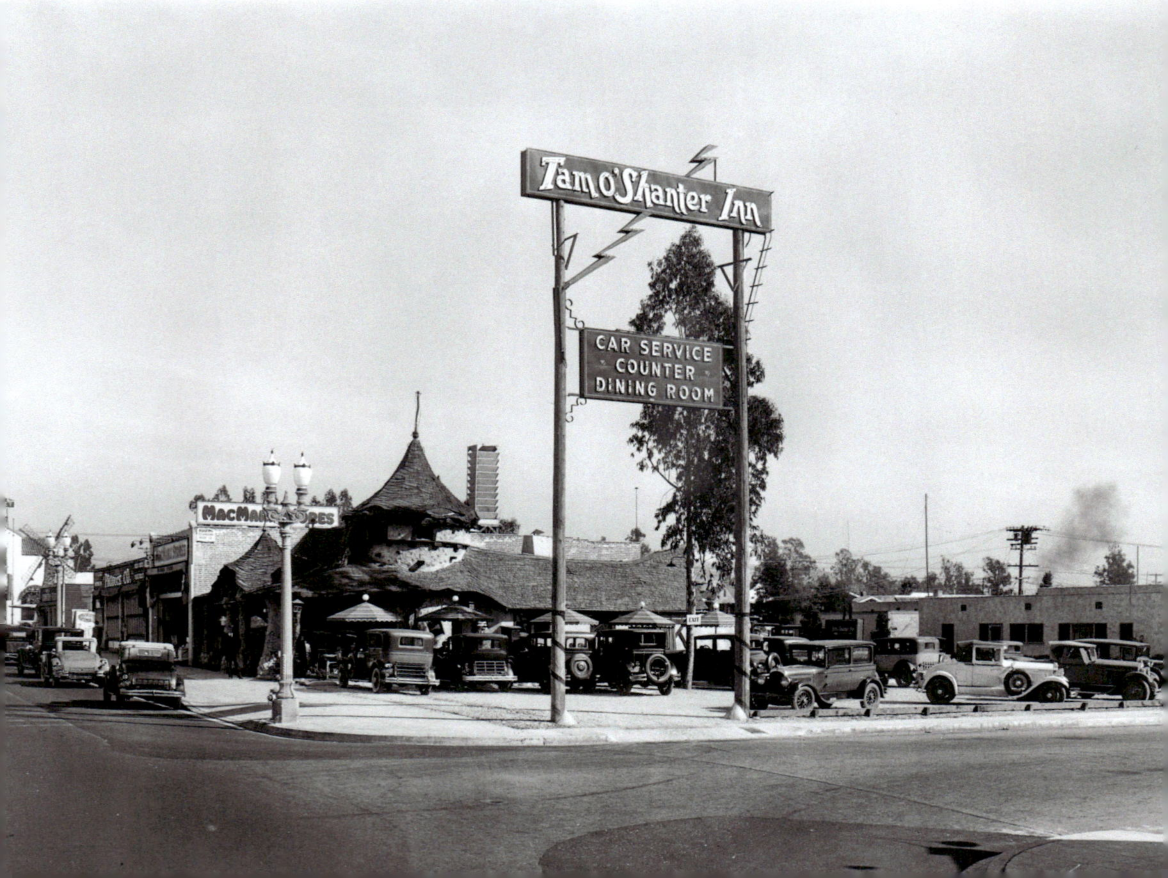
Tam O'Shanter Inn
CAR SERVICE
COUNTER
DINING ROOM

OPPOSITE TOP
Tam o' Shanter Inn matchbook, ca. 1931

OPPOSITE BOTTOM
Tam o' Shanter Inn, 2980 Los Feliz Boulevard, Los Angeles, ca. 1934. Architect: Harry Oliver. Owners: Lawrence Frank and Walter Van de Kamp

ABOVE
Tam o' Shanter Inn, Los Angeles, ca. 1922

LEFT
Tam o' Shanter Inn napkin, ca. 1941

BELOW
Tam o' Shanter Inn, 2980 Los Feliz Boulevard, Los Angeles, ca. 1932

Tuesday – July 26, 1927

# Tam o'Shanter Inn

"A bit o' bonnie Scotland"

## OUR BIG SPECIALS

### HOT TOASTED SANDWICHES

Special Garnish

| | | | |
|---|---|---|---|
| Hamburger, with Bacon | 25 | Baked Ham | 35 |
| Salisbury, with Bacon | 25 | Baked Ham and Egg | 45 |
| Hamburger with Egg | 35 | Fried Egg | 20 |
| Hamburger Club | 50 | American Cheese—Toasted | 25 |
| Chicken Club | 75 | Frankfurter (extra quality) | 15 |

### COLD SANDWICHES

| | | | |
|---|---|---|---|
| Chicken | 60 | Swiss Cheese | 20 |
| Chicken Salad | 50 | American Cheese | 20 |

Trilby (Raw Hamburger ..... 25

NOTE.—Our Hamburger and Salisbury Meat is ground here five or six times daily from choice cuts of fresh round steak. If you're "from Missouri" and want to be shown, we'll be pleased to show you our kitchens, the quality of the meat we use, and our electric grinder.

(OVER)

ABOVE
Tam o' Shanter Inn postcard, ca. 1931

RIGHT
Tam o' Shanter Inn menu, 1927

SANDWICHES 10¢
MENU

MALTED MILK AS YOU LIKE'EM
THE TAMALE
HAMBURGERS · HOT TAMALE PIE · CHILI · SPANISH DELIGHT · TAMALES
6421

The Tamale, 6421 Whittier Boulevard, Montebello, ca. 1930. Owner: H. W. Lane

MALTED
MILK
AS YOU LIKE'M

ENCHILADAS

OPPOSITE AND RIGHT
The Tamale,
6421 Whittier Boulevard,
Montebello, ca. 1928

BELOW
Charley's Beauty Salon,
6421 Whittier Boulevard,
Montebello, 2000

FOLLOWING SPREAD
TeePee Barbecue,
5231 East 2nd Street,
Long Beach, ca. 1931

FO

TAIN

COCKTAILS
THE TEE PEE
Where Braves and Squaws Gather for Fun
GOOD FOOD - DRINKS - MUSIC
Most Original Rendezvous in Long Beach
5251 East Second Street
Long Beach, Calif.

OPPOSITE
The TeePee menu, ca. 1931

ABOVE
TeePee Barbecue, 5231 East 2nd Street, Long Beach, ca. 1931

RIGHT
TeePee Barbecue advertisment, ca. 1932

JUDGE RAYMOND J.
ARATA
PERIOR COURT
9

MUSIC
ACCORDIONS

THEODORE
SCHOOL of MUSIC

PREVIOUS SPREAD AND OPPOSITE
Theodore School of Music,
1666 Union Street,
San Francisco, ca. 1950.
Owner: Theodore Pezzolo

BELOW
Theosophical Society,
Point Loma, ca. 1905

LEFT
Toed Inn advertisement, ca. 1944

BELOW
Toed Inn, 140 West Channel Road, Santa Monica, ca. 1931

OPPOSITE TOP
Toed Inn menu, ca. 1947

OPPOSITE BOTTOM
Toed Inn, 12008 Wilshire Boulevard, Los Angeles, ca. 1940

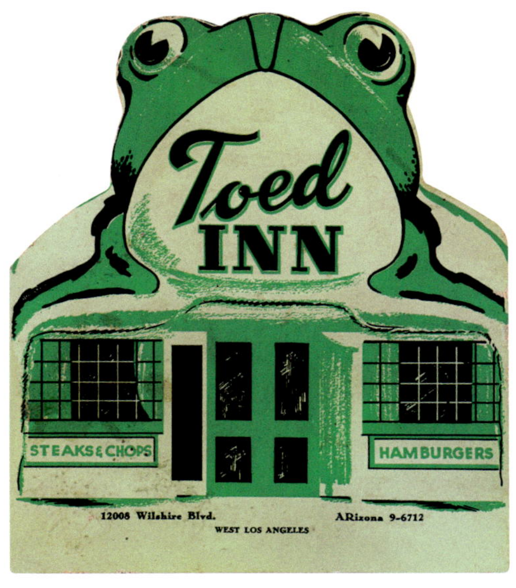

Toed
INN
STEAKS & CHOPS
HAMBURGERS
12008 Wilshire Blvd.
WEST LOS ANGELES
ARizona 9-6712

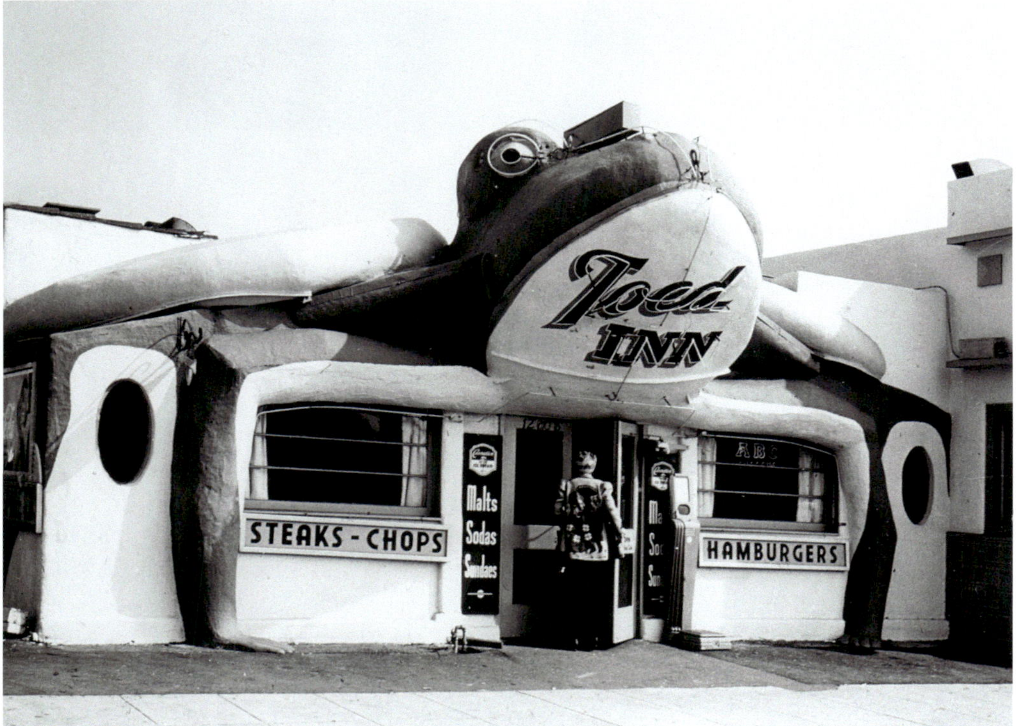
Toed
INN
STEAKS - CHOPS
Malts
Sodas
Sundaes
HAMBURGERS

ABOVE
Toonerville Trolley,
1635 West Manchester Avenue,
Los Angeles, 1930

LEFT
Toonerville Trolley matchcover,
ca. 1930

OPPOSITE
Toonerville Trolley,
1635 West Manchester Avenue,
Los Angeles, 1920

TOONERVILLE
Free Coffee
TAMALES
CHILI
HOT DOGS
TOONERVILLE TROLLEY
SANDWICH
ICE CREAM
SODAS

BELOW
Tower Auto Court,
11580 Ventura Boulevard,
Studio City, ca. 1932

OPPOSITE
Tower Auto Court brochure,
ca. 1937

LOS ANGELES
EAT
Tower
AUTO COURT
HOLLYWOOD

OPPOSITE TOP AND BOTTOM
Tug Boat House,
Pacific Coast Highway,
Trancas Beach, ca. 1932

BELOW
Tug Boat House,
Pacific Coast Highway,
Trancas Beach, ca. 1940

BELOW
Twin Barrels, 7200 Beverly Boulevard, Los Angeles, 1931

OPPOSITE
Twin Barrels, 7200 Beverly Boulevard, Los Angeles, 1930

TRIPLE
XXX
Carnation

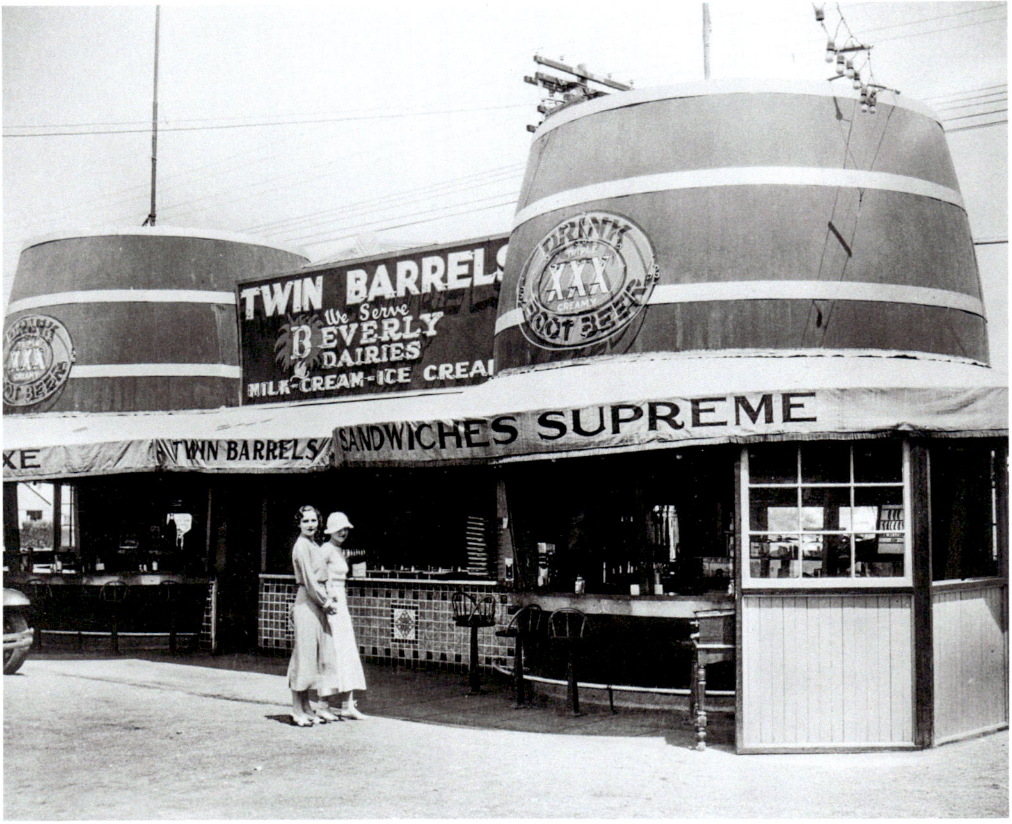
TWIN BARRELS
We Serve
BEVERLY
DAIRIES
MILK-CREAM-ICE CREA
DRINK
XXX
ROOT BEER
SANDWICHES SUPREME
TWIN BARRELS

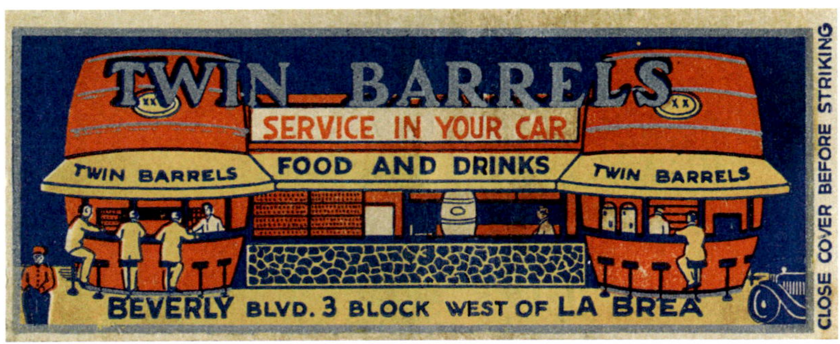

TWIN BARRELS
SERVICE IN YOUR CAR
TWIN BARRELS
FOOD AND DRINKS
TWIN BARRELS
BEVERLY BLVD. 3 BLOCK WEST OF LA BREA
CLOSE COVER BEFORE STRIKING

OPPOSITE TOP
Twin Barrels, 7200 Beverly Boulevard, Los Angeles, ca. 1932

OPPOSITE BOTTOM
Twin Barrels matchbook, ca. 1932

RIGHT
Joseph P. Murphy Super Service Station, 830 South La Brea Avenue, Los Angeles, ca. 1930

BELOW
Twin Boat Apartments, 390 West F Street, Encinitas, ca. 1928. Architect/builder: Miles Kellogg

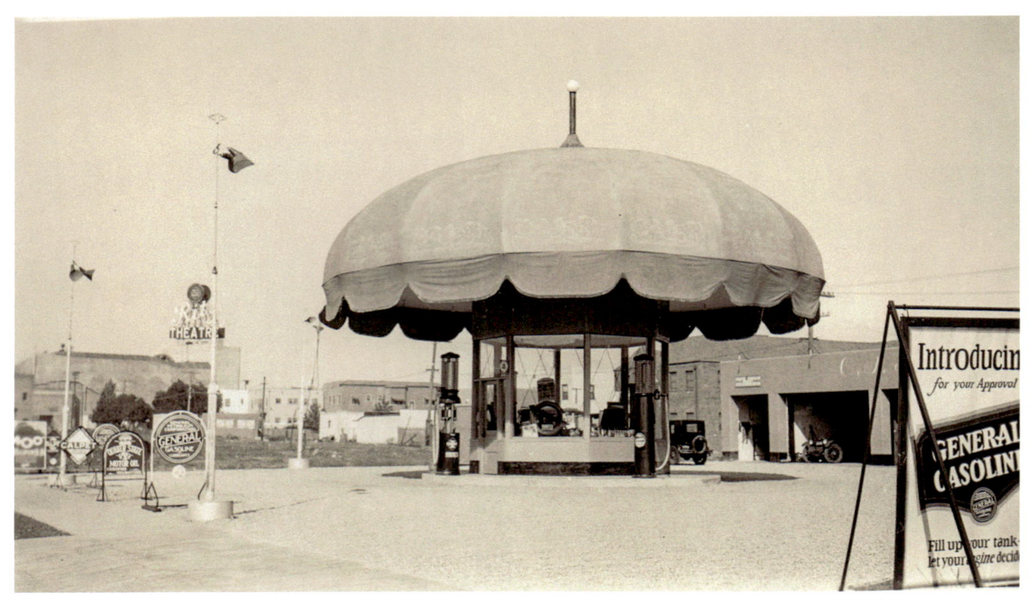

THEATRE
CALPET
GENERAL
GASOLINE
Introducin
for your Approval
GENERAL
GASOLIN
Fill up your tank
let your engine decid

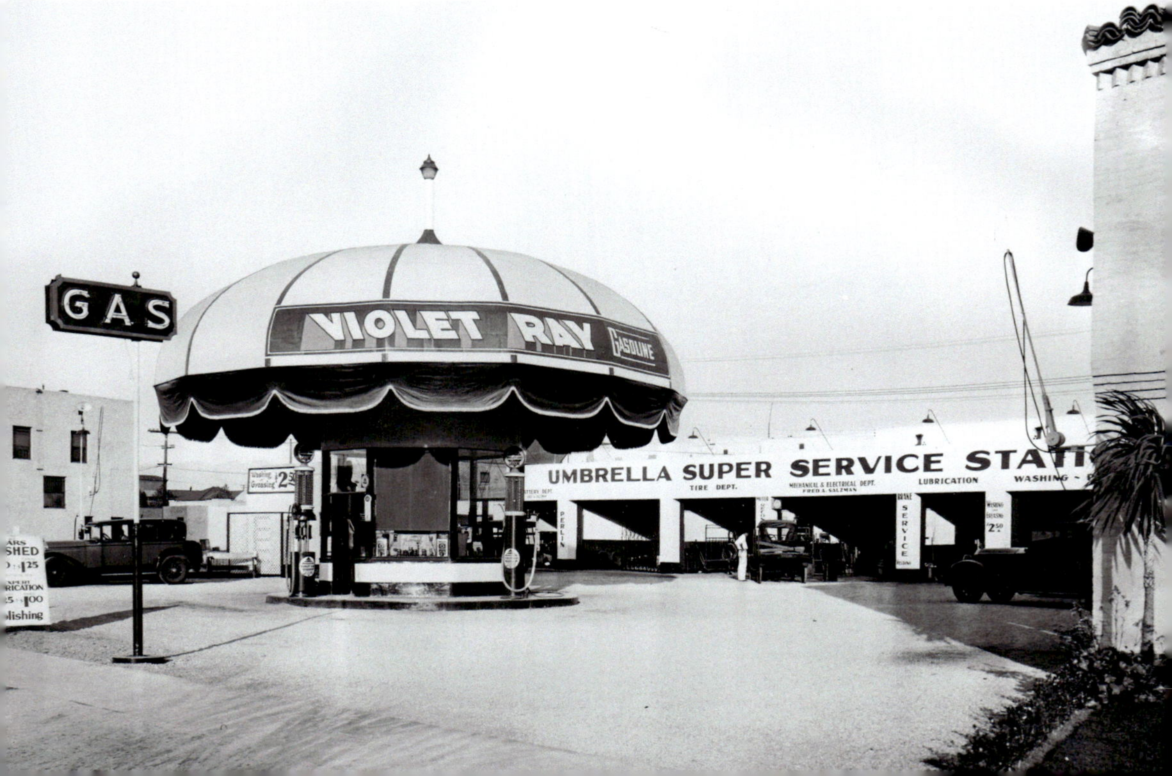
GAS
VIOLET RAY
GASOLINE
UMBRELLA SUPER SERVICE STATI
TIRE DEPT.
MECHANICAL & ELECTRICAL DEPT.
FRED A. SALZMAN
LUBRICATION
WASHING
PERLIN
BRAKE
SERVICE

OPPOSITE TOP
Umbrella service station, 830 South La Brea Avenue, Los Angeles, ca. 1928

OPPOSITE BOTTOM
Umbrella Super Service Station, 830 South La Brea Avenue, Los Angeles, ca. 1932

RIGHT
Upside Down Boat matchcover, ca. 1935

BELOW
Upside Down Boat, Oxnard, ca. 1935

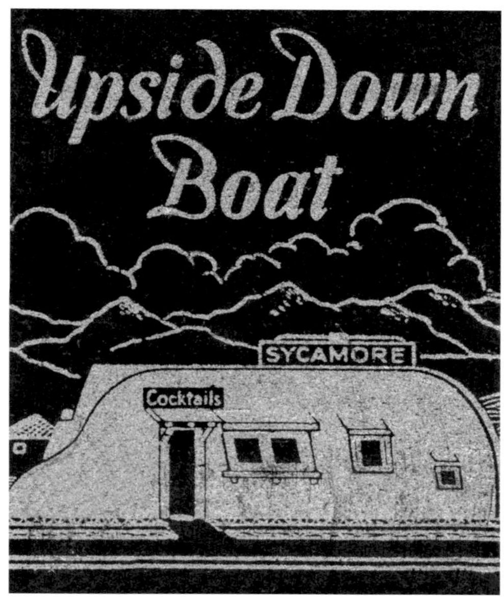

BELOW
United Equipment, 600 West Glenwood Avenue, Turlock, ca. 1980

OPPOSITE
Van de Kamp's, Los Angeles, ca. 1926

de Kamp's
KERS
LOOK FOR THE MILL
ASK FOR
Holland Dutch
COFFEE
CAKES

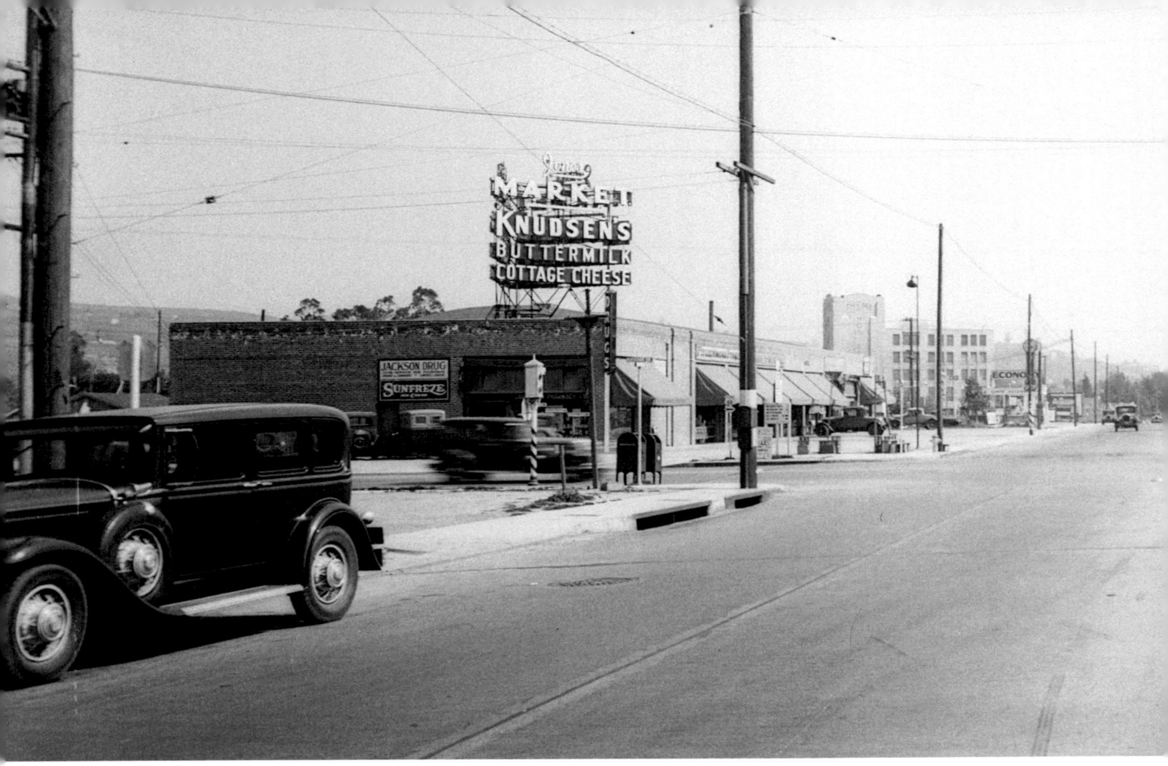
MARKET
KNUDSEN'S
BUTTERMILK
COTTAGE CHEESE
DRUGS
JACKSON DRUG
SUNFREZE

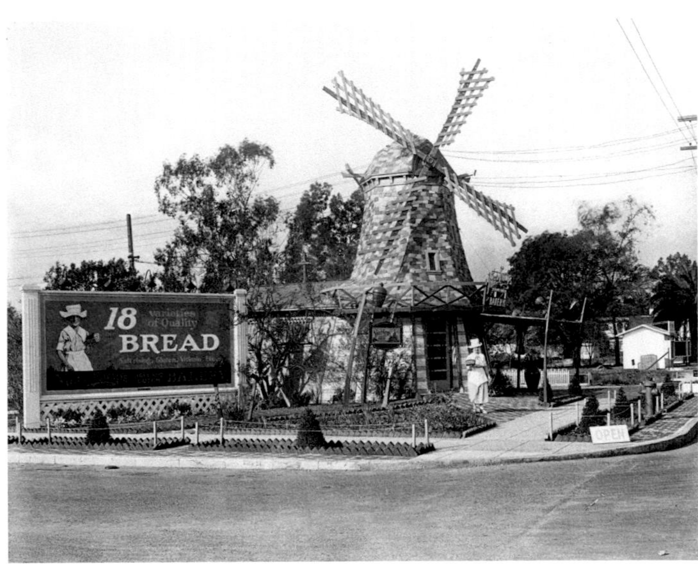

18
varieties of Quality
BREAD
OPEN

ABOVE
Van de Kamp's, Fletcher Drive and San Fernando Road, Los Angeles, 1932

OPPOSITE
Van de Kamp's, Glendale, ca. 1925

RIGHT
Van de Kamp's Bakery, Los Angeles, ca. 1925

WESTWOOD
OBSERVATION TOWER

OPPOSITE
Westwood Observation Tower, Wilshire and Beverly Glen Boulevards, Los Angeles, ca. 1924

THIS PAGE
White Log Tavern, Los Angeles, ca. 1932

ONE
TAGE LIGHTS
ONLY 6 MG TAR
TONY'S
FOOD TO GO
CLOSED
BREAKFAST Special
3 SAUSAGE OR 3 BACON AND 2 EGGS
1.89
TONY'S Special Menu
BEEF TERIYAKI
BAR-B-Q
PORK STEAK
SHRIMP TERIYAKI
TABLISHED IN 1948
11th
Your world. It's all here.

OPPOSITE
Tony's Burgers, 1061 South Hill Street, Los Angeles, ca. 1976

BELOW
White Log Tavern, Los Angeles, 1943

LEFT
Indian Village Café menu,
Arcadia, ca. 1926

BELOW AND OPPOSITE
Wigwam Orange Stand,
1457 Huntington Drive, Arcadia,
ca. 1926

LEMONS
5¢ Doz

OPPOSITE TOP
Wigwam Indian Village, 1457 Huntington Drive, Duarte, ca. 1928

OPPOSITE BOTTOM
Wigwam Indian Village, 1457 Huntington Drive, Duarte, ca. 1936

RIGHT
Wigwam Indian Village, 1457 Huntington Drive, Duarte, ca. 1921

BELOW
Wigwam Indian Village, 1457 Huntington Drive, Duarte, ca. 1926

FOLLOWING SPREAD
Wigwam Village, 2728 East Foothill Boulevard, Rialto, ca. 1952

OPPOSITE
Wigwam Village, 2728 East Foothill Boulevard, Rialto, ca. 1954

ABOVE
Wigwam Village, 2728 East Foothill Boulevard, Rialto, ca. 1950

RIGHT
Wigwam Village, ca. 1949

LEFT
Spadena House, 516 Walden Drive, Beverly Hills, 1991

BELOW
Willat Studio, 6509 West Washington Boulevard, Culver City, ca. 1922. Architect: Harry Oliver

OPPOSITE
Wilshire Links, Wilshire and La Cienega Boulevards, Los Angeles, 1930. Owner: Mary Pickford

Wilshire Links, Wilshire and La Cienega Boulevards, Los Angeles, 1930. Owner: Mary Pickford

Hamburger
15¢

Wilshire Links, Wilshire and La Cienega Boulevards, Los Angeles, 1930. Owner: Mary Pickford

ABOVE
Wilshire Links, Wilshire and La Cienega Boulevards, Los Angeles, 1930. Owner: Mary Pickford

OPPOSITE TOP
Wimpy Burger, 14317 Valley View Avenue, Santa Fe Springs, 1986

OPPOSITE BOTTOM
Wing Co., 1041 East Colorado Street, Pasadena, ca. 1949

FOLLOWING SPREAD
Zamboanga, 3826 West Slauson Avenue, Los Angeles, 1940

1041 E. Colorado St. PASADENA, CALIFORNIA
WING CO.
..RCA VICTOR..TV...
WING-CO
1041
1047
KTTV
11
KLAC
13
KHJ
9
KNBH
4
RCA VICTOR
RCA Picture Power

JOE'S
ZAMBOANGA
ZAMBO
HOME
TAILLESS
SLAUSON AVE.

ANGA
KEYS
HAL DIXON
BUILDING CONTRACTOR
CHARLSTON 6-4393

ABOVE
Zep Diner matchcover, ca. 1931

BELOW AND OPPOSITE TOP
Zep Diner, 515 West Florence Avenue, Los Angeles, ca. 1931

OPPOSITE BOTTOM
Zep Diner business card, ca. 1931

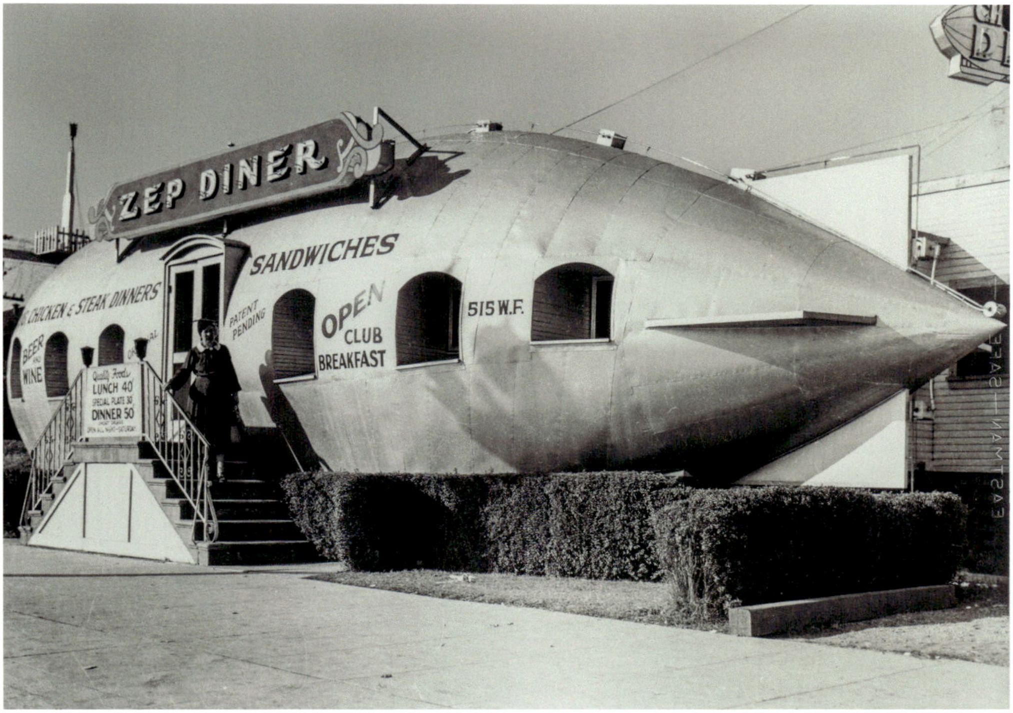
ZEP DINER
SANDWICHES
CHICKEN & STEAK DINNERS
PATENT PENDING
OPEN
CLUB
BREAKFAST
515 W.F.
BEER
WINE
LUNCH 40¢
SPECIAL PLATE 30¢
DINNER 50

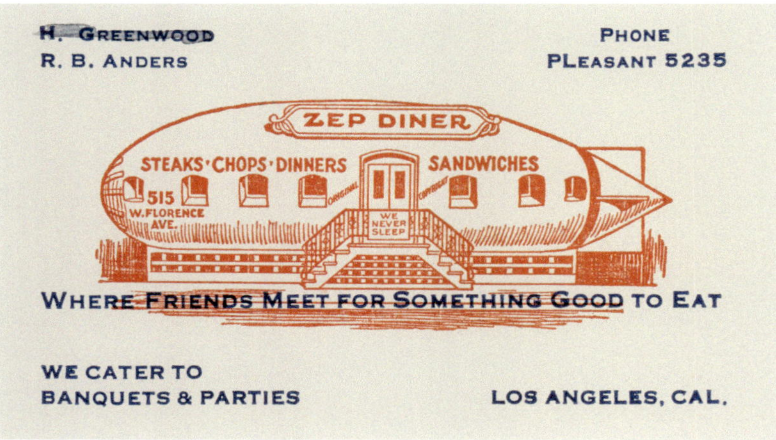

H. GREENWOOD
R. B. ANDERS
PHONE
PLEASANT 5235
ZEP DINER
STEAKS·CHOPS·DINNERS
SANDWICHES
515
W. FLORENCE AVE.
WE NEVER SLEEP
WHERE FRIENDS MEET FOR SOMETHING GOOD TO EAT
WE CATER TO
BANQUETS & PARTIES
LOS ANGELES, CAL.

RAYMOND McKEE'S
ZULU HUT
STOP IN
VISIT ZULU HUT
HALF MILE BEYOND THE TURN TO
UNIVERSAL CITY ON VENTURA BLVD.
for BEST FRIED CHICKEN AND SQUAB
OPEN TILL 2 A.M.
$1.10 EVERYTHING

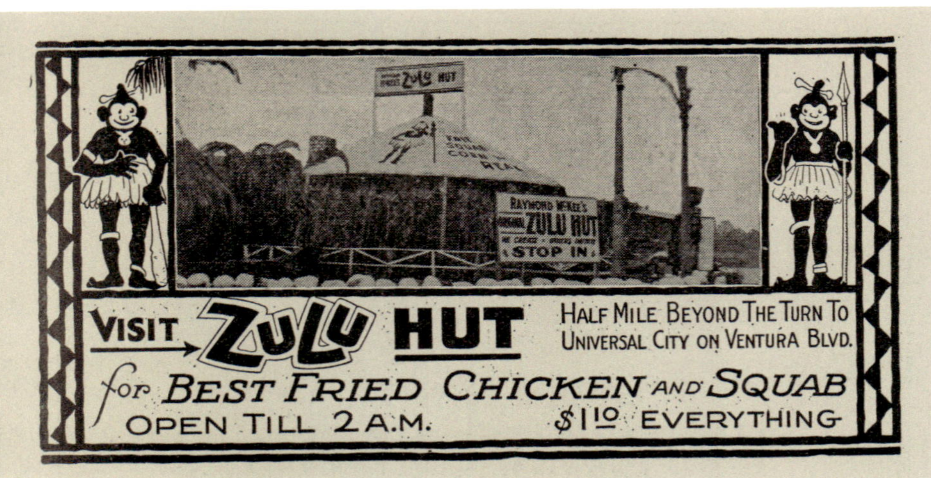

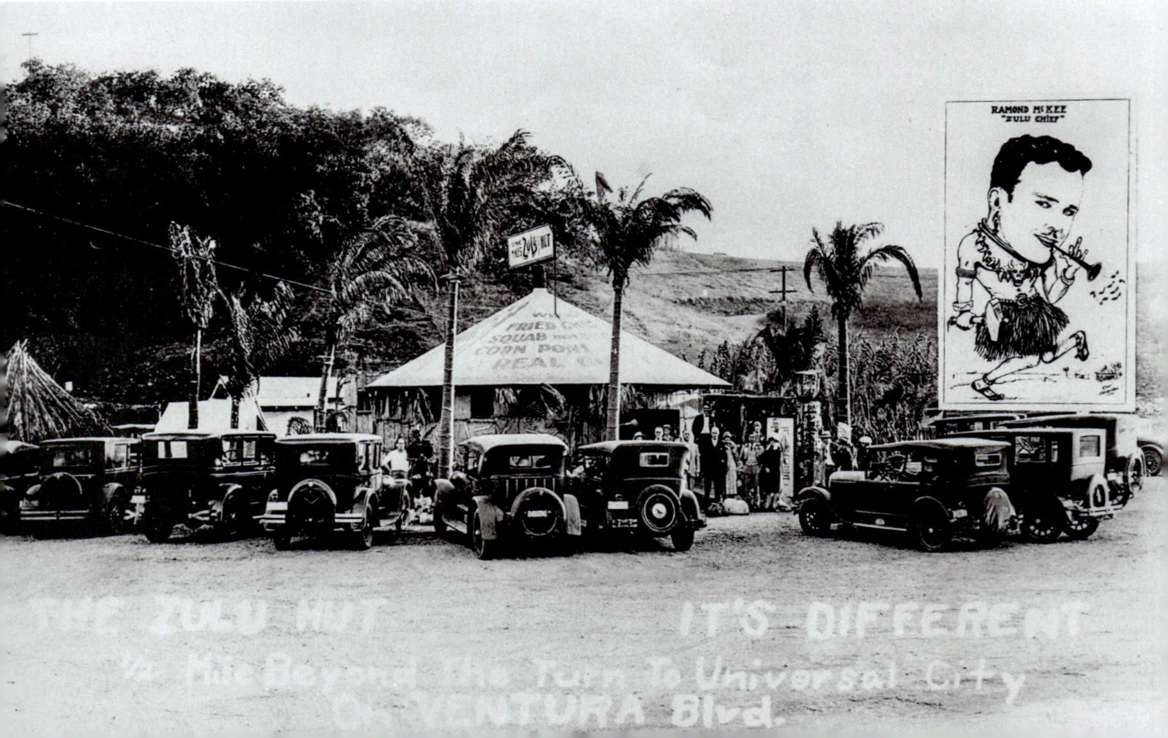
RAMOND McKEE
"ZULU CHIEF"
FRIED
SQUAB
CORN PONE
REAL
THE ZULU HUT
IT'S DIFFERENT
½ Mile Beyond The Turn To Universal City
On VENTURA Blvd.

OPPOSITE TOP
Zulu Hut advertisement, ca. 1927

OPPOSITE BOTTOM
Zulu Hut, 11100 Ventura Boulevard, Studio City, ca. 1928

ABOVE
Zulu Hut, 11100 Ventura Boulevard, Studio City, 1925

FOLLOWING SPREAD
Entrance to Beverly Crest real estate development, Los Angeles, 1926

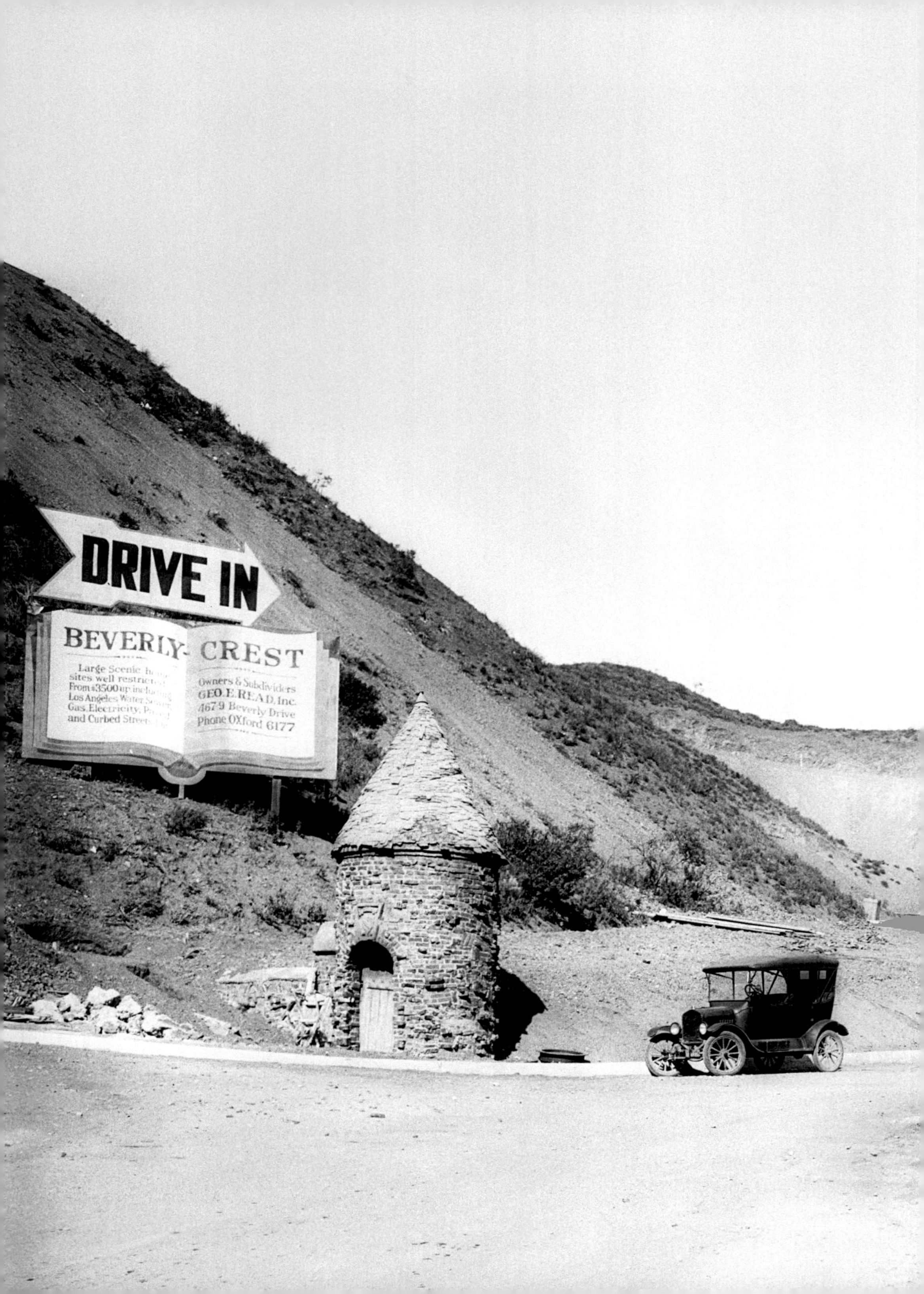
DRIVE IN
BEVERLY-CREST
Large Scenic
sites well
From $3500 up
Los Angeles Water
Gas, Electricity,
and Curbed
Owners & Subdividers
GEO. E. READ, Inc.
4679 Beverly Drive
Phone OXford 6177

# WEIRD ARCHITECTURE HELPS TO SELL ICE CREAM

Southern California Has Taken the Lead in Producing Weird and Novel Roadside Stands, of Which These Are Examples

Strange Beasts and Birds, Enormous Mushrooms, and Replicas of Milk Cans, Ice-Cream Cones and Other Artificial Objects Are to Be Seen on Every Hand by the Tourist

Even Gigantic Figures Molded of Concrete, Whose Spreading Skirts Shelter the Stock in Trade, the Clerks and the Customers, Sprout Up, with Their Gay-Colored Awnings, along the Concrete Highways

# A Lasting Architecture

by David Gebhard

"If, when you went shopping, you found you could buy cakes in a windmill, ices in a gigantic cream-can, flowers in a huge flowerpot, you might begin to wonder whether you had not stepped through a looking glass or taken a toss down a rabbit burrow and could expect Mad Hatter or White Queen to appear round the next corner. But there would be nothing unreal about it if you were in Hollywood, South California, for shops of that kind are to be seen in all the shopping districts there."

This reaction by a Briton in the late 1930s is just one of many times Southern California has been viewed as the land of exotica. From the 1870s on, that which has seemed startling and unique in the Southland has been cultivated by both natives and visitors so that myth has slowly become fact.

In the late 19th century the exotica of Southern California almost always cited were its tropical and semi-tropical vegetation and what seemed to be a looser, more carefree mode of daily life. By the mid-1880s the exuberance (or, as some felt, madness) of its architecture was added as another California oddity. In the early 1900s California as a place distinct from the rest of the United States became a major theme in its literature, arts, and architecture. California's drippingly sentimental cultivation of the Mission Revival in architecture, followed by its passionate, indeed almost religious, conversion to the Spanish Colonial Revival in the 1920s, were broad-scale efforts to make the contrast between it and the American East and Midwest as sharp and as startling as possible.

It could well be argued that the high point of California's image as the land of the unique was directly tied to the emergence of California as Automobile-Land. In addition to providing the means to realize suburbia, that greatest of American ideals, the automobile encouraged an entirely new way to experience the built or planted environment. California's mild climate, which allowed structures to be erected cheaply and quickly, encouraged a nonserious view of not only architecture, but symbolism and salesmanship as well. Why not make the process of selling and buying as lighthearted and enjoyable as aspects of the free living which California had made possible?

PAGE 428
*Popular Mechanics* article, 1928

LEFT
Futuristic building prototype, ca. 1765. Architects: Étienne-Louis Boullee and Claude-Nicolas Ledoux

OPPOSITE
Elephant of the Bastille, Paris, 1831

And if Californians were going to be fully committed to this "auto-mania" (as it was called in the 1910s), then why not cultivate a set of architectural images which would instantly catch the eye, and which we would continue to remember? Driving by or attending a motion picture showing in Los Angeles at Grauman's Chinese Theatre (Meyer and Holler, 1927) or at the Egyptian Theatre (Meyer and Holler, 1922) or at the Mayan Theatre (Morgan, Walls, and Clements, 1927) was not an experience easily forgotten. Equally, a run by a tire manufacturing company posing as an Assyrian palace (Samson Tire and Rubber Co.; Morgan, Walls, and Clements, 1929) was a far more effective way of pressing us to remember the product than a series of roadside billboards.

The introduction of the automobile made possible the horizontal spread of Los Angeles with its resulting low density, and low land values, and in the process it brought about the development of a wide range of auto-oriented drive-in architecture. California — and Los Angeles in particular — did not originate auto-oriented signage and architecture, but its physical environment, its lifestyle, and its degree of commitment to the automobile made its fulfillment possible in the Southern California scene. As the New York–based editors of *The Architectural Forum* noted in an article, "Palaces of the Hot Doges," published in 1935, "anything haywire is always most haywire in California."

The quantity of spoken and written verbiage devoted to high art painting and sculpture published in the last century has often led us to respond to their symbolic intent rather than their purely visual image. The truth is that the museum label, scholarly art historical slide presentation, or coffee table monograph on a major artist often seems greater than the object itself.

Except for a high art small elite, architecture has not yet experienced a similar wholesale transference of values from the world of symbolism. So far the middle-class audience has not been pressed to first read an explanation of a building and

VAUXHALL
HAVE YOU SEEN THE INDUSTRIOUS FLEAS
ON FRIDAY
VOTE FOR
ARE YOU AWARE YOUR HAT IS VERY SHABBY
ENGLISH OPERA HOUSE
EXTRAORDINARY HIT
LAST DAYS OF
POMPEII!
JERUSALEM
COMET!
OPEN
VESTRIS
PARIS
FAVORITE
HARLEY
THE SLAVE
JOHN PARRY
Grand Concert
ADELPHI
ROBERT MACAIRE
THE CHRISTENING!!!
OBERON
SHAVING
CHESTER
TWO LECTURES
BULL MOUTH!!!
THE DESTRUCTION OF POMPEII EVERY EVENING

OPPOSITE TOP
Poster hoarding, *A London Street Scene*, 1840. Artist: John Parry

OPPOSITE BOTTOM
Moulin Rouge Elephant, Paris, ca. 1900

RIGHT
Colossal Elephant of Coney Island, 1885

then go out and experience it. This is not to imply that direct and indirect symbolism does not exist in buildings, but rather that the visual language generally employed within the Western European architectural tradition has been a popular coinage generally understood by most members of society. In the 20th century, the architectural language of the Colonial Revival, English Tudor, French Norman, or Classical Beaux Arts was, through its historical allusions, direct and understandable. Equally, buildings which were clothed in the garb of the new, ranging from the Art Nouveau, to the Zigzag (Art Deco) and Streamline Moderne, to the International Style (Modern), were addressed to a wide audience, ranging from the architectural elite to the middle class. In most instances these buildings might well reveal layers or symbolic subtleties understood by only a few, but a knowledge of these subtleties was not necessary for a middle-class American to respond to the essential symbolism.

If we glance back to history and examine the European inheritance in architecture, we will find that the symbolic intent displayed by buildings can (with just a little squeezing here and there) be placed in several different pigeonholes. The largest of these would accommodate the time-honored tradition of architectural borrowings or plagiarism from architecture's own past. The use of past architectural languages to comment on both the past and present is an overriding quality of the classical tradition of Greece and Rome. Equally, the direct and indirect borrowings experienced during the medieval period, and thence the Renaissance to the present moment, illustrate how the European tradition of architectural borrowing has been its dominant, most consistent theme.

A second, much smaller, pigeonhole would hold symbolic borrowings which lie outside the realm of traditional architectural language. These exterior borrowings range from the zoological and botanical

LEFT
Creation ride, Louisiana Purchase Exposition, St. Louis, Missouri, 1904

OPPOSITE
Sphinx head, ca. 1923

forms to those taken from the idealized realm of geometry, such as spheres and squares. The entrance to a garden grotto through the mouth of a river monster, a multistory dwelling built as an elephant, a spherical house, or, in the 20th century, an enlarged hot dog as fast-food restaurant are programatic devices meant to convey a set array of meanings. As with traditional architectural borrowings, the non-architectural images may well be resplendent with architectural meaning; still, they were meant to be readable by those who were to experience and use them.

Finally there is another category of architectural borrowings that should be housed in its own tiny pigeonhole: These are those employing either elements of traditional architecture vocabulary or nontraditional forms to convey meaning by indirection. In the English Picturesque Garden tradition of the 18th century, the miniature classic temple, the exotic Islamic kiosk, or the ruins of a medieval castle played a game of double transference. We're not being asked to respond to them in a straightforward fashion as examples of conventional architectural imagery; rather, their intent was to comment on the present and its relation to the past.

In the 20th century, a hotel built as an Aztec temple or an enlarged ice cream cone used to sell ice cream employed similar elements of indirect symbolism. While the English Picturesque Garden was limited in its audience to the gentry who could read its meaning, such was not the case with most nontraditional architectural imagery in the 20th century.

Before looking into the history of our nontraditional architectural borrowings it would be well to see if we could catalogue them in some fashion. The word "programatic" could be suggested as a possible all-embracing term to describe this specified approach to architectural language. The vocabulary employed in these buildings hinged on a program organized to convey meaning by indirection. The program of intent and the visual means

[Entered at the Post Office of New York, N. Y., as Second Class Matter.]

A WEEKLY JOURNAL OF PRACTICAL INFORMATION, ART, SCIENCE, MECHANICS, CHEMISTRY, AND MANUFACTURES.

Vol. LIII.—No. 2.] [NEW SERIES.] NEW YORK, JULY 11, 1885. [$3.20 per Annum. [POSTAGE PREPAID.]

### THE COLOSSAL ELEPHANT OF CONEY ISLAND.

The reputation that the American people have long had of always doing everything on the grandest possible scale, has received lately a very substantial confirmation in the two monuments that have recently been bestowed upon this country. The Washington Monument and the statue of Liberty are the greatest works of art in height and magnitude that have been raised by the hands of man since the Tower of Babel. In addition to these there is a third monument, facetiously styled the eighth wonder of the world, that has recently been raised in the neighborhood of New York, that for one reason deserves to be,named in the same connection with the foregoing, namely, on account of its size. The Colossal Elephant at Coney Island has not been favored with much serious public attention, owing to the fact principally that it is not an artistic work, and secondly, because it is the project and property of a stock company, whose unexalted aim was to rear a structure that would serve, not so much to elevate the public mind artistically, nor to stand as a monument to some of our noted forefathers, but rather to abstract the unwary dime from the inquisitive sightseer. This fact, and the grotesque nature and enormous size of the colossus, has deprived it, up to this time, of much consideration, but this should not deter us from inquiring how a building of such unique design and original construction was called into being.

It was designed and built under the personal supervision of the architect, Mr. J. Mason Kirby, of Atlantic City, N. J. It was first intended to make it a hotel, but later this idea was abandoned, and it was decided to construct the interior with the purpose of using it as an auditorium for concerts, etc., while the platform on the top, or the howdah, as it is termed, would serve as

(*Continued on page* 21.)

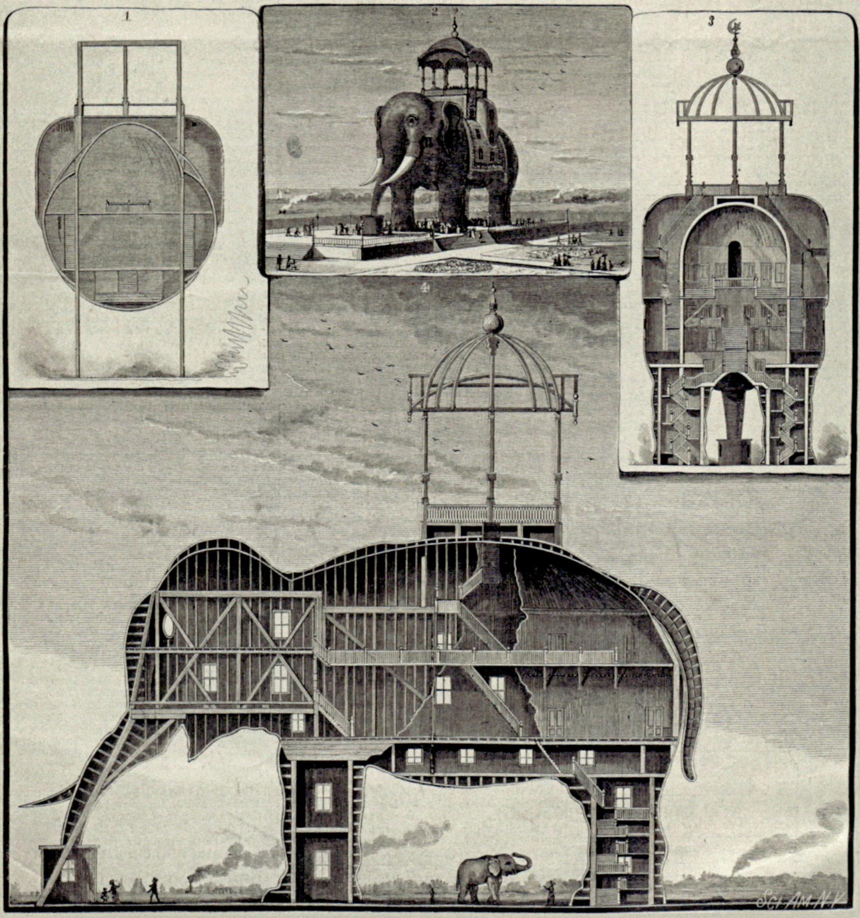

THE COLOSSAL ELEPHANT OF CONEY ISLAND.

OPPOSITE
*Scientific American* magazine cover, 1885
RIGHT
Ingersoll's Luna Park, Cleveland, Ohio, ca. 1906

employed were integral with one another. The audience, then, was being asked to respond not to the artifact, but to the programatic utterance lying behind the form. In traditional architectural borrowings, by contrast, the means (style or fashion) employed had an existence in its own right, regardless of other meanings which might be ascribed to it.

Programatic borrowings of the past can be divided into two basic sources: those emanating from the world of high art and those derived from low art. Within European tradition the principal low art examples have been signs to advertise and sell services and merchandise. For the literate as well as an illiterate audience a hanging sign in the form of a boot was a far more effective way of letting us know that this was a shoe shop than using the written word. A sign in the symbolic form of the product was a well-used device not only in the Middle Ages, but also in ancient Rome, and it has continued as a mode of communication right down to the present.

Alongside this programatic, one-to-one symbolism has been another convention of employing signs which expressed the name of the establishment. An inn named "The Head of the Horse" might well advertise its presence by a cutout, slightly sculptured sign in the form of a horse's head. In the 19th century the scale of these programatic signs was greatly increased. Large sculptured forms might surmount or be placed in front of a building, directly or indirectly indicating its usage. As a case in point, in the 1890s the Eleventh Street Branch of the Grand Central Market in Oakland, California, boasted a fully sculptured, brightly painted cow three times the size of a real cow.

A second source from the European past came out of the high art world of architecture and landscape architecture. The villa gardens of Imperial Rome confronted their visitors with fountains and grottos often in the form of real and mythical animals, humans and plants. Topiary — the sculpting of vegetation in the forms of these and

LEFT
Advertising pedestal for Richfield gasoline, 7786 Santa Monica Boulevard, Los Angeles, 1929

OPPOSITE
California Piano Supply Co., 2251 Venice Boulevard, Los Angeles, ca. 1932

other exotica—was another time-honored tradition. Pliny the Younger, writing of his own garden at Tusculum, speaks of trees "cut into a variety of shapes." The Roman tradition of topiary continued on through the Middle Ages, and it was utilized with renewed enthusiasm during the Renaissance. In the 16th century and later, the specific symbolic Roman use of garden structures in the form of fantastic humans and animals came once more into play. It crept into the urban environment, where in the 1593 Palazzo Zuccari in Rome, visitors entered the palazzo through the mouth of an anxiously awaiting monster.

High art's principal contribution to Programatic architecture occurred in the late 18th century in the English Picturesque Garden tradition and in the work at the end of that century of the classical visionary architects. These architects pursued three versions of Programatic architecture. Their dominant commitment was to the world of geometry transformed—transformed in scale and put to factual and symbolic uses. Claude-Nicolas Ledoux's often-illustrated Quarters for the rural caretakers of the 1780s, in the form of a freestanding sphere, disassociated from the landscape, is an example which immediately comes to mind. The sphere, symbolic of geometry, could also be enshrouded with an overlay of other meanings. Étienne-Louis Boullée's memorial to Isaac Newton (1784) used the sphere to symbolize the Newtonian view of the universe, while Ledoux employed the sphere in his Plan for a Cemetery (1773–79) to evoke a sense of death and the underworld. These French, German, English, and American visionary architects employed a full package of programatic tricks to yank us out of the world of everyday reality. Traditional architectural elements and parts of buildings were raised to a scale diverging from reality. Forms were borrowed from man's real or mythical past or from the faraway worlds of China, India, and the Near East. Buildings which borrowed entirely nontraditional architectural imagery

CALIFORNIA PIANO SUPPLY CO.
ENTRANCE

included Ledoux's Woodcutter's House and Workshop (1773–79), in the form of a pyramidal stack of wood; Boullée's Cenotaph for a Warrior (undated), where we were confronted with a classical sarcophagus which had been blown up into a large building; and finally Jean-Jacques Lequeu's Barn in the Form of a Cow (undated).

The 19th century continued this high art tradition of Programatic architecture in only a marginal way. Certain pure geometric forms, such as the octagon, enjoyed great popularity, but the programatic exoticism of this form became so watered down in fact and symbolic content that most people of the time responded to it within its own advertised realm of supposed rationalism and utility. By the 1880s, the exoticism of non-European architectural languages — Islamic, Chinese, and Japanese — had become so commonplace in the way they were used that they could only be marginally thought of as Programatic.

In contrast, the popular 19th century scene provided a much stronger continuity between the distant past and the 20th century. Signage — in scale, lavishness, and sheer quantity — put the pre-1800 world to shame. Nowhere was this more true than in the United States, where by the end of the century immense thirty- to forty-foot billboards were erected in towns and cities. Anticipating the billboards was the convention of painting signs directly on the walls of buildings; in the later half of the 19th century this practice was expanded so that entire walls of commercial buildings and rural barns were transformed into giant advertising signs.

An important link in the upward and inward progress of Programatic buildings was a few structures in the form of elephants and other creatures, the most widely known being James V. Lafferty's come-on "Lucy the Elephant" built at South Atlantic City (now Margate), New Jersey, in 1881. Lafferty's sixty-five-foot creation was modeled on the designs of the French

OPPOSITE
Chili Bowl, 3141 Cahuenga Boulevard, Los Angeles, ca. 1937

RIGHT
MacPherson's Drive-In, Long Beach, ca. 1940

architect Charles-Francois Ribart for a garden kiosk in the form of an elephant, which were published in 1758. Ribart's creatures served as a symbol of the triumphs of the French crown; Lafferty's 19th-century elephant sold real estate.

Around the turn of the 20th century there was an increase of Programatic buildings in amusement promenades of national and international expositions and in a growing number of amusement parks. The impact of these buildings tended to be somewhat different, for they existed in a non-everyday environment: Their visual amusement or shock was minimal compared to what happens when these unfamiliar forms pop up in our everyday world.

During the 20th century the introduction of the automobile promoted a new wave of direct Programatic architecture. Not only did the automobile encourage the Programatic, it could even participate in its spirit as in 1911 when the California Corrugated Culvert Company of San Francisco had its company car built in the form of a corrugated culvert, which happened to have an engine and four wheels. The use of enlarged sculptured products to sell, which had begun in the 19th century, was raised to new heights both physically and symbolically in the first two decades of the 20th century. In Indianapolis, a milk company constructed two fifty-foot-high milk bottles of glazed bricks, and other smaller-scale milk bottles, beer jugs, and wine bottles began to appear along America's developing systems of highways. During the next two decades, the 1920s and '30s, the many forms of Programatic architecture were firmly ensconced on the scene. Though there were examples built on the Continent and in England, it was the United States, and especially the West Coast, which brought forth most of the examples.

The popular version of the modern, the Zigzag Moderne (Art Deco) of the '20s and early '30s, introduced Programatic elements into its buildings. In the gem of the Moderne — the Chrysler Building in

LEFT
Pasadena, ca. 1936

OPPOSITE
Warner Bros. Theatre, 9404 Wilshire Boulevard, Beverly Hills, 1930

New York (1930)—architect William Van Alen established a Programatic decorative program of "glorifying American mechanical genius and incidentally Mr. Chrysler's output of cars, trucks, and boats," wrote Kenneth M. Murchison in *The American Architect* in 1930. Radiator caps and emblems were used for flagpole sockets and "on the thirteenth story, the brick-work wheels revolved under horizontal mudguards..." Murchison continued. In Los Angeles, the Sunset Towers, one of the city's major contributions to the Moderne (Leland A. Bryant, 1929–31), helps us to locate the enclosed parking garage by placing terra cotta automobile fronts below and above the windows.

The exponents of the Moderne maneuvered themselves even closer to the pretenses of high art in their frequent use of programatic sculpture. Sculpture depicting historic individuals from classical and nonclassical sources was a favored device of the European and American Beaux Arts tradition from the 1890s through the 1930s. But such figures demanded some degree of humanistic erudition so that the audience could fully comprehend what was supposedly symbolized. The elaborate sculptural program worked for the Nebraska State Capitol Building in Lincoln by Bertram Goodhue, the philosopher Hartley Burr Alexander, and the sculptor Lee Lawrie added the remote highfalutin reference to the past expected of a public building, but because of its limited audience this approach could certainly not be used to sell an everyday product of American industry. As a rule, the popular architectural sculpture of American Moderne generally assumed a more programatic approach. The four tympanum figures over the entrance to Los Angeles' black and gold Richfield building (Morgan, Walls, and Clements, 1928) symbolized Aviation, Postal Service, Industry, and Navigation—all, of course, powered by oil. These classically inspired figures were made understandable (it was hoped) by adding wings and a propeller to the figure

WARNER
BROS.
WARNER
BROS.
CHARLIE CHAPLIN IN "CITY LIGHTS"
BOBBY JONES IN "HOW I PLAY GOLF"

HOLLYWOOD
FLOWER
POT

OPPOSITE
Hollywood Flower Pot, 1100 North Vine Street, ca. 1932

RIGHT
Garden of Eden, ca. 1936

of Aviation, and by attaching similar easily recognizable appendages to the other three figures.

The play between innuendoes of high art and direct programatic art was a theme which occurred with moderate frequency in roadside advertising of the 1920s. The serious-minded lamented what they saw happening to the roadside. With the completion of an extensive portion of the national highway system by the early 1930s the advantages of regional and national repetitive highway signage came into the picture. The most extravagant of these were the sequential Burma Shave signs with their quizzical utterances luring the driver to the final Burma Shave sign, and sign notices throughout the upper Midwest leading to Wall Drug Store in Wall, South Dakota. The image of the Burma Shave signs was fitting for a national product while the Wall Drug Store signs had an appropriate fallen-down Western look.

The California architect Robert H. Orr noted that the way things were going, "our highways, byways, and street corners will be lined with sculptural monuments rivaling those strewn along the 'Holy Way' to the ancient Tombs of the Kings." Orr was referring to three-dimensional sculptural advertising signs usually consisting of a high base which bore the written message, and sculptural horses and riders, bulls, or racing cars placed on top. In some instances there was an understandable relationship between the sculpture above and whatever it advertised, as the figure of the bull helped name Ye Bull Pen Inn in Los Angeles, or a depiction of Barney Oldfield and his racing car helped sell Richfield gasoline. In other instances, "famous" statuary was taken from the world of high art with seemingly no direct connection (other than the prestige of "Art") between the sculpted figure and the advertising product. The inventiveness of programatic signage was especially evident in the 1930s. In 1931, the Coca-Cola Company used real-life female models to sit under make-believe palm trees to enjoy the "pause that refreshes."

EAT
LADIES

OPPOSITE
Patent drawings, 1930s–1940s
RIGHT
Wm. Penn Dining Room, U.S. 13 and U.S. 40, Wilmington, Delaware, ca. 1925

The play between that which is and that which is not was frequently employed in large billboards when real objects occurred within an illusionary painted sign. The General Sign Company of Oakland placed a coupe from the Howard Motor Company within a tropical island setting complete with a sunset, and on the roadside outside of Milwaukee there was a real yellow-and-silver airplane, apparently crashing into the ground. This eye-catcher let the passing motorist know it was only a twenty-minute drive to a Schuster's Department Store. A subtle, complex interchange between the real and the illusionary occurred in a large sign in Indianapolis, where a gigantic make-believe mirror enlarged a moving sequence of views of the individual shops located in the Circle Tower shopping center. In this instance the signage with its movement accentuated by changing colored lights existed as an intermediator between the potential customer and the actual passage into the individual shops.

Another 20th-century link with the Programatic architecture of the past is to be found in the use of architectural imagery which was either exotic (the faraway or distant past), or was a perversion of some past European architectural mode; forms we would loosely label as "medieval" were a favorite imagery of the 1920s. But this medieval imagery was meant to be read through our remembrances of the fairy-tale world of Hansel and Gretel. These little witches' cottages—which might serve as real estate offices, service stations, or fast-food restaurants—play an intriguing game with scale and other make-believe elements. They are, in fact, dollhouses enlarged, but kept at a distance from the world of traditional imagery.

The range of non-European traditional imagery utilized during the '20s reveals that through popular magazines (especially *The National Geographic* for the American middle-class audience) the world architectural scene was just waiting to be grabbed up. The rash of 18th- and

19th-century non-European borrowings was continued, although the context was meant to be more jarring, so that their indirect message could be more favorably conveyed. Egypt, Babylon, Assyria, Japan, China, and Hindu and Islamic India provided vocabularies for anything ranging from restaurant interiors to motion picture theaters. Added to these older borrowings was a new group of "primitive images" derived from the Pacific world of Melanesia and Polynesia, the pre-European pueblos of the American Southwest, the teepees of the Plains Indians, and the Pre-Columbian architecture of the Maya, the Zapotec, and the Aztec of Mexico and Central America.

During the '30s these exotic borrowings were joined and almost overwhelmed by the imagery of the Streamline Moderne. The Streamline Moderne, as a popular architectural system of imagery, seized the element of speed — epitomized in the aerodynamic design of the airplane — and applied it to the full range of designed products, including signage and large and small buildings. Even signs were caught up in the Streamline urge: "If outdoor advertising is to keep its foremost place among advertising mediums it must keep its foremost place in design, too, along with motor cars and airplanes and railroad trains," opined *Signs of the Times* magazine in 1935. That which distinguishes the Streamline Moderne has to do with how the audience was asked to respond to the building. In the case of a Streamline Moderne building the audience was expected to see it as architecture which had been clothed in modern garb. Programatic Streamline Moderne buildings exist in the form, for example, of a streamlined train as a diner, a streamlined boat as a restaurant, or a streamlined automobile as a service station. By the end of the 1930s the Streamline Moderne image, with its hint at what glories lay in store for us in the future, had almost entirely supplanted the older languages of Programatic architecture.

An illustration of how the '20s could be tied to the '30s and how the past could

OPPOSITE
The Wigwam, Adrian, Michigan, ca. 1933

RIGHT
A & W Root Beer, 4203 East Central Avenue, Albuquerque, New Mexico, ca. 1950

be linked to the future can be seen in the many fast-food hamburger shops in the form of streamlined castles. The single corner tower used for the chain of White Tower hamburger shops was all that was needed to suggest that it was medieval. The Wichita-based White Castle buildings played off the hygienic image of white porcelain panels against a crenelated parapet and tower, while the Tulsa-based Silver Castle chain ended up with a totally streamlined box which retained its allegiance to the medieval past solely through its name and logo.

Turning our attention specifically to California's Programatic architecture of the 1920s and '30s, it is of interest to note that these Programatic forms came onto the scene late in the '20s and more of them were built during the opening years of the Great Depression than before. Though there were examples before 1928, their high point was between 1928 and 1934. This is borne out not only by examples which were constructed but by the numerous unbuilt examples for which patents were issued. The ingenuity of American designers is pointedly and delightfully revealed in the array of "impossible" visual images which they patented; what was built in California and elsewhere reveals only the tip of the iceberg in terms of America's faith in the Programatic to sell services and products. Lunch pails, jugs, teapots and cups, locks and keys, corncobs, milk bottles, ice cream cones and freezers, birthday cakes, icebergs, soup bowls, oranges, hot dogs, and tamales were joined by dogs, pigs, and dancing girls as constructions. There also were machine themes applied to buildings: airplanes, ships, automobiles, and even spark plugs and light bulbs.

If we apply our earlier categories to these examples, buildings and signs generally fall into two basic groups: those whose imagery directly conveys what was being sold, and those which employed a wide variety of indirect messages to advertise. All of the Programatic structures, whether a

tamale stand built in the form of a tamale or a service station shaped like an airplane, were created to be eye-catchers: They were meant to startle, shock, and amuse. Humor was an essential element in the audience's response to these structures. Even the streamlined passenger car as a diner, with its allusions to the future, was meant to convey a sort of lighthearted Buck Rogers excursion.

Direct Programatic architecture — the structure as a sign of what it was selling — succeeded because of the simplicity of its symbolism, whereas indirect Programatic architecture entailed degrees of meaning which, one suspects, had the potential of holding the audience's attention for a longer period. An enlarged hot dog from which hot dogs were sold exemplifies a first step in the process of injecting indirect meaning into the architectural vocabulary. An iceberg to sell cold soft drinks and ice cream or a restaurant built as a teapot or coffeepot suggests that this is a place where food and drink may be obtained. A service station in the shape of an airplane asks that the audience symbolically connect two machines with the selling and consuming of energy-producing products.

All of these buildings somehow manage to maintain connections between the form of the structure and what is being advertised, but such is not the case for a wide variety of exotic languages which often occurs in Programatic architecture. An owl enlarged to a small building which houses an ice cream stand reveals no connection between the product and the form of the building. Perhaps, it might be suggested, there is linkage to be found in the childhood world of fairy tales, reinforced in the '20s and '30s by the dream world of the Hollywood motion picture. The architectural garb provided in Los Angeles by Grauman's Chinese Theatre, the Egyptian Theatre, and the Mayan Theatre was openly employed to carry the theater-goer into an intermediary non-everyday world, and thence into the visual mythology of the film. The far distant lands of the Egyptians,

OPPOSITE
Mushrooms Café, 3500 West Olive Avenue, Burbank, ca. 1927

RIGHT
Coffee Pot, 7275 Beverly Boulevard, Los Angeles, 1936

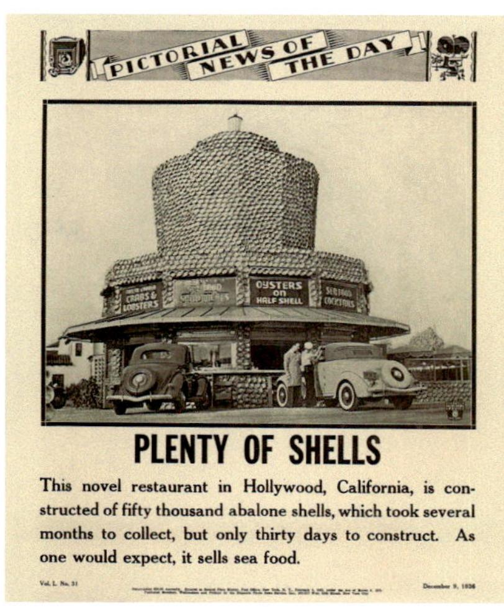


PICTORIAL NEWS OF THE DAY

PLENTY OF SHELLS

This novel restaurant in Hollywood, California, is constructed of fifty thousand abalone shells, which took several months to collect, but only thirty days to construct. As one would expect, it sells sea food.

Vol. I. No. 31 December 9, 1936

of the Mayans, and the Chinese were, by the mid-'20s, a more effective device to carry the audience into the film than the earlier use of the sumptuous Beaux Arts baroque.

The most prevalent building types associated with Programatic architecture were those associated with the automobile and drive-in architecture. Here the need for quick identification at a reasonable speed and distance meant that a building which could catch the eye could or should draw in customers. In writing about Pasadena's well-known Mother Goose Pantry (1929), which was built as a great shoe, a writer noted that "[Colorado] Boulevard is lined with wayside places of various types and designs for miles. Every one of these is forgotten, however, save the famous Mother Goose Pantry."

A theme which enjoyed great popularity throughout the United States was that of the frontier log cabin. One of the earliest of these in California was the ca. 1911 Old Log Cabin refreshment stand in San Diego. Numerous variations on this theme were carried out in California in the 1920s and 1930s, including buildings in the form of a single tree trunk. In 1930 the log cabin was seized upon as an architectural style for a chain of small fast-food restaurants, the White Log Taverns. The first of these was built in Oakland, and by 1937 there were sixty-two of these fast-food restaurants located throughout California. The White Log Taverns, with their frames of steel sheathed in concrete logs, played off two sets of images: that of a log cabin and that of the American Colonial Style. For a national image, this added up to the best of two worlds. Another California example of the virtues of the American home and the frontier was the Big Fireplace restaurant in Los Angeles (1927), which greeted its customers with two giant-scale exterior fireplaces augmented by a pattern of ever-changing red lights. The parking lot and the street had become one great big living room.

More indicative of the California scene, and especially of Southern California, was

BELOW
Mother Goose Pantry, 1959 East Colorado Boulevard, Pasadena, ca. 1929

OPPOSITE
Tony's Burger, 1061 South Hill Street, Los Angeles, 1996

the occurrence of Hansel and Gretel architecture. The first of these buildings on the Los Angeles scene was designed by Harry Oliver, who was a set designer for Metro-Goldwyn-Mayer studios. In 1921 he designed the studio offices for Irvin C. Willat Productions in Culver City. "We have tried," noted Irvin C. Willat, "to reproduce a tumble-down structure of two centuries ago, but which will be equipped with the most modern office appurtenances." The reason for this cultivated architectural exoticism

was no different than that for a drive-in restaurant. A 1921 newspaper article of the time reported, "It is said that this structure has occasioned more comments from passing motorists than any building being erected in Los Angeles in recent months."

Within a year Oliver went on to design the first of Van de Kamp's Bakery's famous shingle-covered windmills, and the Tam o' Shanter Restaurant located on Los Feliz near Griffith Park. The Tam o' Shanter was supposedly California's first drive-in restaurant, and it was the first of the Los Angeles drive-ins to consciously cultivate the world of Alice in Wonderland. Its fairy-tale atmosphere was openly connected at the time to Hollywood: "The Tam o' Shanter Restaurant is the product of movie town architecture efficiently applied," wrote the *Pacific Coast Record* in 1938.

In the late '20s and early '30s, movieland versions of Hansel and Gretel cottages were built throughout the West Los Angeles area, many of them designed by the productive and professionally respected firm of Pierpont and Walter S. Davis. Robert H. Derrah, who is best remembered for his Coca-Cola Company Building in the form of a streamlined ocean liner, employed the Alice in Wonderland theme for his Continental Villa, which formed a segment of his 1936 Crossroads of the World on Sunset. Half-timbered medievalism continued on into the post–World War II years, but these later examples establish their relationship to the traditional world of architectural imagery rather than to the storybook world of Alice or Hansel and Gretel.

In the East, South, and Midwest, the Colonial was by far the favored image for a wide variety of small roadside commercial buildings, ranging from service stations to restaurants. In California the imagery of the Colonial was occasionally used, as in Fatty Arbuckle's Plantation Café of 1928 on Washington Boulevard. In this case, it was the signage on the roof and on the long mound of turf which pulled the structure and its setting out of the normal world of

architecture. That this perversion of the past has not left us is readily apparent in the 1960 Pacific Savings (now California Federal Savings) designed by Rick Farver Associates, where the full-blown visage of George Washington's Mount Vernon has been moved from the shores of the Potomac to a site overlooking the Hollywood Freeway.

More instances of California's Mission, Spanish, and Mediterranean imagery used for small-scale commercial purposes tended to be rather straightforward interpretations of one or another of these modes. Just off the path of traditional architecture were those marginal establishments which employed the Pueblo Revival, the Moorish or Islamic Revival, and the Pre-Columbian of Mexico and Central America. Gay's Lion Farm (1926) in El Monte and, above all, the impossible Cliff Dwellers Café on Beverly Boulevard (1927) illustrate how a non-European architectural image could be pulled into the realm of the Programatic. Equally strained in its relationship to the traditional were a wide array of Islamic-inspired designs: the Calmos #1 service station (1925) on Hollywood Boulevard with its domed mosque-like station accompanied by two minarets, and Roland E. Coate's Calpet service station (1927) on Wilshire Boulevard, where the final touch was the female Moorish attendants who serviced your Packard or Franklin. The Islamic theme was employed for King's Tropical Inn on Washington Boulevard (1926), which somehow sought to connect its specialty chicken dinners with the exotic world of Africa and the Near East. In the '30s the imagery of the Land of the Arabian Nights encouraged an Iranian mosque for the Beverly Theatre (1930–31) and for the extensive offices of the Girard Real Estate Development (1928) on Ventura Boulevard.

While the downtown Mayan Theatre was locally the most widely known of Los Angeles' pre-Columbian exercises, the most extensively written about was Robert Stacy-Judd's Aztec Hotel (1926)

OPPOSITE
Hollywood Flower Pot, 1100 North Vine Street, ca. 1933

BELOW
Aztec Hotel, 311 West Foothill Boulevard, Monrovia, ca. 1925. Architect: Robert Stacy-Judd

in Monrovia. The delightful and at times humorously mad maneuvering of historic images can be seen if we compare the Oriental theme of the Mandarin Market (1929) on Vine and Grauman's Chinese Theatre, or the Egyptian assertions of Glendale's Egyptian Village Café (1924) and the Egyptian Theatre in Hollywood.

*come in! . . . tune in!*

# TONIGHT

## GRAND OPENING SANDERS SYSTEM

*drive-in sandwich shops**

BRILLIANT PROGRAM OF OUTSTANDING TALENT OFFERED FOR YOUR APPROVAL

AT

7275 BEVERLY BOULEVARD, Leo Forbstein and his entire Vitaphone recording orchestra will be our guests and will radiocast by remote control over station KFWB from 8:00 to 10:00 p. m.

AT

202 N. VERMONT AVENUE, the famous Hollywood American Legion band will entertain you from 8:00 to 11:00 p. m.

AT

1950 WEST WASHINGTON BOULEVARD, you will be entertained all evening by popular Radio and Stage Stars.

• • • • •

There will also be entertainment novelties and surprises at each Sanders shop throughout the entire evening.

Remember — If you cannot come in . . . . tune in! This program will be the outstanding broadcast of the day!

## SIT AND EAT IN YOUR CAR

*LEO FORBSTEIN . . . and his entire Vitaphone recording orchestra in person at the opening of the Beverly Blvd. shop.*

Look for the sandwich shops with the giant coffee pot on top. These shops are the only ones in the city with complete soda fountain service in connection. Those who wish to sit at tables will find here the only drive-in sandwich shops with plenty of booth space inside. Soon you will find these sandwich shops everywhere . . . but now, to secure this superior service, you must drive to the locations shown below.

**Sanders System Drive-In Sandwich Shops can be easily distinguished by the giant coffee pot on top . . . a trade mark that stands for highest quality foods, cleanliness and superlative service.*

*HOLLYWOOD AMERICAN LEGION BAND . . . This world famous military band will entertain you with stirring airs Fri. and Sat. evenings.*

With the opening of the first three Sanders System Drive-In Sandwich Shops (there'll be 46 within the year), you will be able to sit in your car and be served the same quality food that characterizes the most exclusive downtown restaurants.

You'll be impressed by the instant courteous service, unusually appetizing food and immaculate cleanliness.

. . . . . . . . . . . . . . 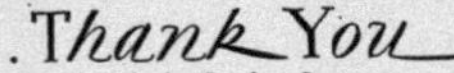


These representative firms have cooperated with the Sanders System to give you the finest drive-in service in Southern California.

Allen Supply Co. (Cudahy Meats)
American Biscuit Co.
American Sign Co.
Anderson Blow Pipe Co. (Mfrs. of Giant Coffee Pots)
Arora Products, Inc. (Neon Signs)
A. Godfrey Bailey (Architect)
J. Baumgarten & Co. (Chili & Tamales)
F. Brahn (Artistic Painter)
Calif. Desk Co.
Calif. Dairies, Inc. (Sunfreze Ice Cream)
Chenoweth & Whitehead (Attorneys)
Christopher Candy Co.
Coffee Products of America, Ltd. (Ben-Hur Coffee)
Dorman Hotel Supply Co. (Full Hotel Equipment)
Electric Refrigeration Sales Co. (Servel Refrigerators.
Favorite & Peterson (Remington Cash Registers).
Four S Baking Co. (Bread & Rolls)
Gelfand Distrib. Co. (Relish & Mayonnaise)
Globe Slicing Machine Co.
Henning & Seiderberg (Brick Masons)
Hollywood Dry Corp. (Ginger Ale and Pomo)
Hollywood Pie Shop
Geo. J. House & Sons (Soda Pop and Eastside)
Kemper Radio Corp.
E. Ward Koch (Contractor & Engineer)
La Brea Mortgage & Investment Co.
Livingston Fancy Foods Products Co. (Cheese, Weiners, etc.)
L. A. Rubber Stamp Co.
National Linen Supply Co.
Purity Bonded Products Co. (Fountain Syrups)
Puro Filter Co.
Sierra Electric Co.
Siller's Paint & Varnish Co.
W. Vaughn Scott (Exclusive Real Estate Agent)
Scudder Food Products Co. (Mayflower Potato Chips)
Standard Ice Co.
Stationers Corp.
Superior Macaroni Co.
United Plumbing Co.
Weber Showcase & Fixture Co. (Fountains & Fixtures)
Yost-Linn Lumber Co.

# SANDERS SYSTEM

S·S

1950 WEST WASHINGTON BLVD
727 BEVERLY BOULEVARD
202 NORTH VERMONT AVENUE

46 MORE "SANDERS SHOPS WILL OPEN IN LOS ANGELES WITHIN THE NEXT YEAR

OPPOSITE
Coffee Pot advertisement, Los Angeles, 1930

RIGHT
Big Duck, West Main Street, Riverhead, New York, 1931. Owner: Martin Maurer

A recurring theme in 18th-century architecture was the return of the primitive, symbolized by the wooden thatched hut. Primitive or indigenous architecture was also played upon as a theme in Programatic architecture of the '20s and later. These images ranged from colorful Arab tents used to sell tropical fruits and juices, to thatched restaurants offering South Seas cuisine. The theme with the widest popular appeal was the Plains Indian teepee. Here was a form which was closely tied to the romance of the West. To spend a night in a teepee motel or have one's car serviced at a teepee village was a marvelous way imply a connection between the nomadic Plains Indians, the westward movement of covered wagons, and the automobile and the open highway.

Los Angeles' gift to America of buildings and signage represents a mixed-up world of fact and myth. Promotional trade, popular, and professional publications obviously delighted in illustrating Los Angeles' roadside buildings in the forms of oranges, jugs, and flowerpots. Photographs of these Programatic buildings not only presented startling visual objects to their readers, but there was always the implication that the buildings illustrated were typical of the scene. As artifacts of the roadside scene these Programatic buildings often lack the usual documentation associated with larger, more conventional, buildings. It is unlikely that we will ever know just how many of them were actually built. Altogether there were probably fewer than seventy-five Programatic buildings built in Southern California. What strikes one in looking through the published illustrations of these buildings is that only a small handful — fewer than a dozen — were illustrated over and over again. Generally these were the most flamboyant, though one often has a sneaky suspicion that these were the Programatic buildings which by chance happened to have been photographed. While the Hoot Hoot I Scream ice cream stand in the form of an owl was located on Long Beach Boulevard, this

was not a street which would normally be traveled by the casual visitor to Los Angeles. Thus the implication at the time and later that Los Angeles and Southern California highways and streets were lined by hundreds of Programatic buildings was simply not true.

The chronological history of Programatic buildings in California closely follows the pattern already mentioned in the discussion of traditional architectural imagery. One of the earliest examples was Abbot Kinney's 1903–04 restaurant ship Cabrillo and Venetian Gardens, which was situated on the Venice Pier. This make-believe ship on piles pretended at one moment to be a Spanish galleon; in the next it was a fragment of a Venetian palace. By 1920, the Cabrillo was joined by a small scattering of buildings and three-dimensional signs situated in both Northern and Southern California. An often-repeated theme was the building in the form of a milk bottle, but other exotica — oranges, artichokes, and pumpkins — entered the scene.

The heyday of California's Programatic buildings occurred during the ten-year period from 1925 through 1934. It was in these years that the most famous of the California examples were built: the Hoot Hoot I Scream building (1925); the Brown Derby restaurant (1926); the Sphinx Realty building (1926); the Igloo building (1928); the Tamale building (1928); the Mother Goose Pantry restaurant (1929); The Zep Diner building (1930); the Toed Inn stand (1931); and the Pig Café (1934). While there were a few buildings constructed after 1935 — such as Cobb's Chicken House at the 1939 San Francisco World's Fair—which directly continued this earlier tradition, later Programatic transformations looked almost exclusively to the Streamlined Moderne image of the transportation machine for sources. In Los Angeles, Robert H. Derrah's streamlined ocean liner for the Coca-Cola Company Building (1936) was the grandest example, while all that was needed was a set of tracks for the streamlined train engine of

OPPOSITE
Wigwam Motel,
2728 West Foothill Boulevard,
Rialto, 1979

RIGHT
Willat Studios,
6509 West Washington
Boulevard, Culver City, 1922

Alice Faye's Club Car Restaurant (1941) to streak off into the night. The image of the airplane, as the most advanced transportation machine, was employed for service stations, and in 1939 Charlie LeMaire, the Los Angeles restaurateur, patented the Skyline Diner, which was in the form of a Norman Bel Geddes double-decked streamlined airplane. The Dark Room (1938) on Wilshire moves us programatically into the objects sold by employing a streamlined image of a camera as its storefront.

When building activities resumed in California in 1945 after the war, there was almost a complete absence of Programatic buildings: The often-illustrated Tail o' the Pup on La Cienega Boulevard was built or refurbished in 1946, the Wigwam Village in Rialto was built in 1955, along with a few others—just enough examples to indicate that, although low keyed, the tradition was not dead. The image of the doughnut as a symbol for fast food entered the California scene in 1949 with The Big Donut chain, and numerous variations were built like The Donut Hole (1958) in the City of Industry. In more recent years the older Programatic buildings have been joined by The Shutterbug (1977) in Westminster, and by the giant caterpillar as a tractor salesroom in Turlock (1978). There was, though, no break in California's use of Programatic signage between the pre- and post-World War II years. The earlier Programatic signage of a wide-eyed puppy dog which looks down at us from atop Barkies Sandwich Shops (1930–31) was augmented in the postwar period by the giant woman's leg which lets us know that this is indeed Sanderson Hosiery (1948), and by the red-and-white Santa Claus (1950) that announces this is the town of Santa Claus, California.

Variations on this form of architectural signage were large-scale billboards and entire building facades which formed sculptured signs. Clifton's Cafeteria on Olive Street in downtown Los Angeles (1931) with its waterfalls, geysers, and tropical foliage was matched, if not surpassed, by the scene of romping and frolicking pigs which,

in painted and sculpted forms, crawl over the walls and buildings of the Farmer John Meat Packing Plant in Vernon.

The approach taken to language in these Programatic buildings or signage ran the gamut between direct commentary and the exotic. The building in the form of the product sold — a tamale, orange, or lemon — is as obvious as one could ask. The next step of symbolism plays on the theme of the container or mechanism used in the production of the product: the flowerpot as a nursery or flower store, a cream can to sell dairy products, or a hand-cranked freezer to dispense ice cream products. A third set of symbols goes one step further by hinting at some quality associated with the product: an igloo and iceberg to sell cold drinks and ice cream, or a coffeepot to advise the viewer that this is a restaurant.

Then there are those buildings that comment on their names — The Brown Derby, The Toed Inn, or The Pig Café. In such cases there is often an essential need for the Programatic form of the building to be accompanied by written signage so that the potential customer can tie the form and name together. Behind this play between the form and the written word is another element of attraction as to the whys and wherefores of the name itself. The shoe as a building for Pasadena's Mother Goose Pantry restaurant is meant to pull us back into childhood.

But what levels of humorous meanings lie behind such themes as the Round House Café (1927), with its train engine plunging out toward us, or the World War I theme of a crashed airplane and sandbagged trenches of The Dugout (1927) in Montebello? The child's world of the fairy tale certainly lies behind the Mushrooms restaurant (circa 1928) and Pumpkin Palace restaurant (circa 1927), both in Burbank, but other themes like the walled and guarded Jail Café (1926) must somehow appeal to other parts of our sensibilities. The suggestion that there should be a give-and-take between the real, everyday world and some other world

OPPOSITE
Clifton's Cafeteria souvenir photo holder, 1956

RIGHT
Jail Café, 4212 Sunset Boulevard, Los Angeles, 1926

was the overriding theme of California's Programatic excursion into the Streamline transportation machine. In the instances of streamlined ships, trains, and airplanes of the late '30s and early '40s we are asked to hop, skip, and jump back and forth between the then-existing world of technology, the futuristic world of Buck Rogers and Flash Gordon, and the machine-dominated futurism of the 21st century.

Programatic architecture and signage were almost universally condemned by America's upper middle class, professional planners, and the high art world. The first two groups felt (and quite rightly so) that Programatic structures, like billboards and roadside architecture in general, would destroy the City Beautiful sense of order in an urban environment, as well as the sylvan quality of suburbia. They were uncomfortable with the blatant commercialism these structures implied. The proponents of high art were afraid that the frequent use of sculpture in this fashion would debase the original: "Will they not eventually make sculpture…so commonplace that the real object of art cannot, except by those especially trained, be disassociated from the commonplace and cause a decadency far-reaching in its effect and influence?" asked Robert H. Orr in *The Architect and Engineer* magazine in 1927. In a way, of course, this is just what happened. Bit by bit the high art world of Cubism, Futurism, and above all, Dadaism, Surrealism, and Pop has so mixed, transformed, and been transformed, that today a high art aficionado and a good bourgeois will respond with equal ardor to those few remaining vestiges of our Programatic near-past.

It was the foremost of America's architectural historians, Henry-Russell Hitchcock, who as early as 1936 noted that, "The combination of strict functionalism and bold symbolism in the best roadside stands provides, perhaps, the most encouraging sign for the architecture of the mid-20th century."

This affirmative response went basically unheeded and did not reappear until the

OPPOSITE
*Collier's* article, April 6, 1929

PAGE 464
Angel Food Donuts,
15904 Atlantic Avenue,
Compton, ca. 1979

1950s in the pages of *Landscape,* which was founded and edited by J. Brinckerhoff Jackson. Jackson, and the writers he assembled in the pages of *Landscape,* asked us to reassess the whole of our commercial vernacular including the highway and the commercial strip. The imperative which Hitchcock had in mind for Programatic architecture finally arrived in the mid-'60s through the publication of Robert Venturi's volume *Complexity and Contradiction in Architecture,* and in the buildings which he and his associates designed. Venturi's The Big Duck (Martin H. Maurer's roadside stand near Riverhead, Long Island, 1931), symbolizing buildings as signs, brought the whole of Programatic buildings back into high art respectability. Since the early 1970s the Programatic tradition of borrowing from architectural imagery itself and from outside of it has returned with a fervor. In California it seems almost to be a repeat of what occurred in the relationship of the use of programatic forms within the 18th-century English Picturesque Garden tradition and the later occurrence of "real" Programatic buildings. In the 1950s, California began to experience a rash of miniature golf courses resplendent with a wonderful array of toy-sized buildings; by the mid-'70s they began to be supplemented by "real" buildings. Whether the rich treasure trove of California's Programatic buildings will provide a similar inspiration for the future remains to be seen. One hopes it will.

# The City of Make-believe

*The influence of the movie-set builders and carpenters bobs up frequently as you motor along the highways of Los Angeles and environs. They can toss together a monument to anything from a hot dog to a ballroom*

When you drive out to the Brown Derby for a dance and a snack of an evening, there's no danger of missing it. The slightly dizzy architect has seen to that

*All photos by Brown Bros.*

Right: Old Omar did more than help this ballroom out with a name. He conceived a neat little scene to help boost it and all it needed was the coöperation of a skillful plasterer or something of the sort

And lest there be any doubts in your mind as to the exact functions of an up-to-date beach club, they're dispelled by this frolicking group of statuary

And what little boy or girl can guess the name of the delicacy which is handed over the counter to patrons in this circular and unique nook?

ANGEL FOOD
DONUTS
APACHE
COCKTAILS
LIQUOR
APACHE
OPEN

# An Architectural Heritage

by Jim Heimann

Preservation is a dicey business. What is and what isn't historical can be debated ad infinitum. Unfortunately, for many of the buildings in this book, their perceived lack of historical value condemned them to neglect and demolition. For over half a century, critics and the architectural establishment universally dismissed unconventional roadside architecture as ephemeral and a blight on the landscape, an attitude that reinforced their disposal. The buildings themselves often presented a preservation problem. Built on the premise of short-term usage, they were usually constructed of inexpensive materials that would last a decade or so with proper maintenance. If a business flourished it was either enlarged and remodeled or moved to another location where a more substantial building could be built. In the case of Southern California, potential land usage made many sites transitory so their eventual demise was presumed. In other parts of the country, little thought was given to the architectural importance of commercial buildings until late in the 20th century, when preservationists and historical societies began to see value in the recent past. By that time, many of the signature programmatic buildings had disappeared.

There remain some stalwarts out there clinging to their existence by strong lobbying efforts or by dumb luck. Several have fallen victim to misguided preservation attempts by owners attempting to infuse a nostalgic representation onto an authentic building. In an odd twist on reality, several buildings were reconstructed in contained environments or behind theme park walls. The Bulldog Café, for instance, was rebuilt (to earthquake standards) inside of the Petersen Automotive Museum in Los Angeles and another version was installed as a static prop at a Disney theme park. But for structures in the real world, it's a fragile existence. Even in this enlightened age no building is immune to the wrecking ball. The success stories continue mainly due to enlightened individuals who value

LEFT
*Holiday* magazine, January 1950

OPPOSITE
Budget TV Center, 1101 South Western Avenue, Los Angeles, ca. 1972. Photographer: Richard Gutman

retaining the spirit of the original structure. Bar owner and entrepreneur Bobby Green along with his investors successfully saved and pristinely restored the Idle Hour bar, a large oversized barrel, in North Hollywood, California. To complement this landmark they also rescued the Bulldog Café from the Petersen Museum, where it had been scheduled for demolition. The Dog now resides in the patio, two programmatic structures on one site.

Tracking down information about the structures continues to be part of the research process. Some still remain anonymous while several of the more difficult locations came to light after the first edition of *California Crazy* was published. Many buildings were located by long searches through newspaper microfilm, in which ads or real estate announcements gave clues to the locations. Verifying an address or business name magnified from a photo against vintage telephone books and Yellow Pages proved effective in some cases. Match covers, menus, postcards, and brochures continue to be effective research tools.

Interviews with the few remaining building owners reflected something in the human spirit — a desire to express oneself — that resulted in something as concrete as the buildings themselves. This individual expression drove them to build something as outrageous as an oversized pig that dispensed ham sandwiches from its snout.

Tillie Hattrup, the owner of the Hoot Hoot I Scream stand, told the history of her owl-shaped building after having seen her former business in the book. She and her sister wanted a roadside ice cream business and their house, which was situated on one of the major roads entering Los Angeles, was thought to be an ideal location. They enlisted their neighbors, who worked at Hollywood movie studios, to construct an owl for maximum visibility and novelty. Cadillac headlights were installed in the eyes, the neck was made to rotate

and an auto horn blew "Hoot Hoot" periodically. With limited success, the owl was hoisted on a flatbed truck and reinstalled in South Gate near the new Firestone rubber plant. It remained there for over 50 years until it was demolished.

The site of the Hollywood Flower Pot (circa 1930) was discovered when a reader insisted that he knew that the building was on Vine Street just north of Santa Monica Boulevard because he had lived in it. His family, having moved to Hollywood during the Depression, found the flower pot converted to a one-room residence and they promptly moved in!

These stories are evaporating and the historical importance of the structures is in constant flux. New buildings continue to rise, carrying on the tradition with a twist, but once a structure is demolished it often is only recalled in the pages of a book. Hopefully this edition of *California Crazy* will continue to inspire those who seek to preserve the extant buildings and encourage others to build the structures of their dreams. Whatever shape that may be!

CLOCKWISE FROM TOP LEFT

Partially demolished Brown Derby, 3427 Wilshire Boulevard, Los Angeles, ca. 1980

Rebuilt Brown Derby, 3427 Wilshire Boulevard, Los Angeles, ca. 1986

Formerly Tail o' the Pup, San Vicente Boulevard, Los Angeles, ca. 2006

Acapulco Chicken Café, formerly The Burger That Ate L.A., 7624 Melrose Avenue, Los Angeles, ca. 1998

The Burger That Ate L.A., 7624 Melrose Avenue, Los Angeles, ca. 1989

Tail o' the Pup, San Vicente Boulevard, Los Angeles, ca. 1986

TAIL
o'the
PUP
TIME
8512

Dr. SATEY'S

& ADOLESCENT
NIC
PRIVATE
ENTRANCE FRO
PARKING

## BOOKS


Ackley, Laura. *San Francisco's Jewel City*. Berkeley: Heyday, 2015.

Andrews, J. J. C. *The Well Built Elephant*. New York: Congdon & Weed, 1984.

Arbogast, Joan Marie. *Buildings in Disguise*. Honesdale, Pennsylvania: Boyds Mills Press, 2004.

Baeder, John. *Gas, Food, and Lodging*. New York: Abbeville Press, 1982.

Barth, Jack. *Roadside Hollywood*. Chicago: Contemporary Books, 1991.

Barth, Jack, Doug Kirby, Ken Smith, and Mike Wilkins. *Roadside America*. New York: Simon & Schuster, 1986.

Blaisdell, Marilyn. *San Francisciania: Photographs of Three World Fairs*. San Francisco: Marilyn Blaisdell, 1994.

Brownlow, Kevin, and John Kobal. *Hollywood the Pioneers*. New York: Alfred A. Knopf, 1979.

Cirigliano, Linda. *Hoot Mon! The Story of the Tam o' Shanter Inn*. Los Angeles: Lawry's Restaurants, 1995.

Cobb, Sally Wright, and Mark Willems. *The Brown Derby Restaurant*. New York: Rizzoli International Publications, 1996.

Dunlop, Beth. *Building a Dream: The Art of Disney Architecture*. New York: Harry N. Abrams, 1996.

Endres, Stacy, and Robert Cushman. *Hollywood at Your Feet: The Story of the World Famous Chinese Theatre*. Los Angeles: Pomegranate Press, 1992.

Ewald, Donna, and Peter Clute. *San Francisco Invites the World: The Panama-Pacific International Exposition of 1915*. San Francisco: Chronicle Books, 1991.

Fisher, Joan E. *Automobile and Culture*. New York: Harry N. Abrams, 1984.

Hess, Alan. *Viva Las Vegas*. San Francisco: Chronicle Books, 1993.

Gebhard, David. *Robert Stacy-Judd*. Santa Barbara: Capra Press, 1993.

Gebhard, David, and Harriette Von Breton. *L.A. in the Thirties*. Salt Lake City: Peregrine Smith Books, 1975.

Gellner, Arrol, and Douglas Keister. *Storybook Style*. New York: Viking Studio, 2001.

Jenks, Charles. *Bizarre Architecture*. New York: Rizzoli International Publications, 1979.

Kagan, Paul. *New World Utopias*. New York: Penguin Books, 1975.

Keller, Ulrich. *The Highway as Habitat: A Roy Stryker Documentation, 1943–1955*. Santa Barbara: University of California, Santa Barbara, 1986.

Liebs, Chester H. *Main Street to Miracle Mile: American Roadside Architecture*. Boston: Little, Brown and Company, 1985.

Longstreth, Richard. *City Center to Regional Mall: Architecture, the Automobile, and Retailing in Los Angeles, 1920–1950*. Cambridge: MIT Press, 1997.

Longstreth, Richard. *The Drive-In, the Supermarket, and the Transformation of Commercial Space in Los Angeles, 1914–1941*. Cambridge: MIT Press, 1999.

Margolies, John. *Fun Along the Road*. Boston: Bulfinch Press, Little, Brown and Company, 1998.

Margolies, John. *Home Away from Home*. Boston: Bulfinch Press, Little, Brown and Company, 1996.

Margolies, John. *Pump and Circumstance*. Boston: Bulfinch Press, Little, Brown and Company, 1993.

Margolies, John. *Roadside America.* Cologne: TASCHEN, 2010.

Margolies, John. *Signs of the Times.* New York: Abbeville Press, 1993.

Marling, Karal Ann. *The Colossus of Roads: Myth and Symbol along the American Highway.* Minneapolis: University of Minnesota Press, 1984.

Oberhand, Robert. *The Chili Bowls of Los Angeles.* Los Angeles: Robert Oberhand, 1977.

Pennington, Lucinda, and Wm. Baxter. *A Past to Remember: The History of Culver City.* Culver City, 1976.

Peterson, Eric. *Roadside Americana.* Lincolnwood, Illinois: International Publications, 2004.

Phoenix, Charles. *Americana the Beautiful.* Santa Monica: Angel City Press, 2006.

Robideau, Henri. *Canada's Gigantic!* Downsview, Ontario: The University of Toronto Press, 1988.

Sears, Stephen. *The Automobile in America.* New York: The American Heritage Publishing Co., 1977.

Stanton, Jeffrey. *Venice California: Coney Island of the Pacific.* Venice: Donahue Publishing, 1993.

Venturi, Robert, Denise Scott Brown, and Steven Izenour. *Learning from Las Vegas.* Cambridge: MIT Press, 1972.

Weitze, Karen J. *California's Mission Revival.* Los Angeles: Hennessey and Ingalls, 1984.

Williams, Dino, Alexa A. and Greg Williams. *The Story of Hollywoodland.* Los Angeles: Papavasilopoulos Press, 1992.

Williams, Jay. *John Baeder's Road Well Taken.* New York: The Vendome Press, 2015.

## PERIODICALS

Allen, David. "No Guiding Light for Those Adrift in the Desert." *The Sunday Press Dispatch*, Victorville and Barstow, California, March 2, 1997.

Bartolucci, Marissa. "Power." *Metropolis*, December 1994.

Betsky, Aaron. "Cartoon Character." *Los Angeles Times Magazine*, December 18, 1994.

Broersma, Dick. "Lasting Landmarks." *Daily Breeze*, Redondo Beach, California, April 19, 1995.

"California Boom." *LIFE*, June 10, 1946.

"California Sunstruck Signs." *Holiday*, January 1947.

Cardenas, Jose. "All Fixed Up." *Los Angeles Times*, May 25, 1996.

Carroll, Jerry. "Where Did the Giant Orange Go?" *San Francisco Chronicle*, July 29, 1973.

Chamberlain, J. H. "Denver Gets Something Different." *Signs of the Times*, May 1938.

"City May Not Have the Heart for This Building." *Los Angeles Times*, June 15, 1999.

Clinton, Paul. "Inside the Donut Hole." *San Gabriel Valley Weekly*, Pasadena, California, July 3, 1998.

"Colossal Elephant of Coney Island." *Scientific American*, July 11, 1885.

"Complaint Kicks in New Business." *Signs of the Times*, October 1949.

"Crossroads of the World." *California Arts and Architecture*, January 1937.

Dietz, Lawrence. "There Once Was a Woman Who Lived in a Shoe." *West*, November 30, 1969.

Doctoroff, Andrew S. "In Tarzana, Front-End Refinement." *Los Angeles Times*, January 22, 1987.

Ferguson, James. "White Log Taverns." *Pacific Coast Record*, June 1934.

"First Adaptation of Early Aztec Architecture to Modern Structural Designing." *Los Angeles Times*, May 5, 1912.

Godard, Sam F. "From Footlights to Fireplace." *Pacific Coast Record*, June 1927.

"Great American Roadside." *Fortune*, September 1934.

Gregory, Daniel P. "Billboard Buildings." *Sunset*, November 1992.

Graves, Amy Beth. "Tisket, Tasket: Office in a Basket." *Tri-Valley Herald*, Dublin, California, March 2, 1998.

Gutis, Philip S. "Roadside Relics of Early Auto Days Are Being Saved." *The New York Times*, September 3, 1987.

Gutis, Philip S. "Suffolk to Preserve Its Landmark Duck." *The New York Times*, August 26, 1987.

Harvey, Steve. "Eating Away at Oddball Architecture." *Los Angeles Times*, July 20, 1985.

Harvey, Steve. "Only in L.A." *Los Angeles Times*, February 19, 1997.

Heimann, Jim. "Chili Climate." *Los Angeles Magazine*, March 1997.

"How Glorified Ice Cream Stands Advertise and Sell the Product." *The Ice Cream Trade Journal*, March 1928.

Kelly, John F. "Santa Claus." *California Highways and Public Works*, March–April 1956.

Kuck, Lorraine. "Combines Sandwich Shack with Modern Road-House." *Pacific Coast Record*, February 1924.

Lacey, Marc. "Landmark Sign Is Threatened." *Los Angeles Times*, January 11, 1990.

Langdon, Phillip. "The Rebirth of the Bizarre." *Buffalo Evening News*, Buffalo, New York, March 30, 1981.

Laug, Ruth. "That's Entertainment." *Identity*, September–October 1995.

"Marathon Builds Octagonal Station at Tulsa." *National Petroleum News*, August 19, 1931.

Minster, Joe. "Soboba Indian Village." *Pacific Coast Record*, July 1927.

Moore, Kurt. "Ticky, Tacky." *Alaska Airlines Magazine*, April 1989.

"New Faces for Old Novelties." *Nation's Business*, November 1939.

"New Studio Is Novelty, Style Two Centuries Old Copied." *Los Angeles Express*, April 6, 1921.

"Only in Southern California: Claude Bell Builds Himself a Brontosaurus." *People Weekly*, June 23, 1975.

Paper, Henry. "A Hole in One." *California Living*, February 24, 1985.

"Palaces of the Hot Dogs." *Architectural Forum*, August 1935.

Pastier, John. "Chiat's New Look." *Adweek*, November 4, 1991.

"Plastic Statues Supplant Roadside Billboards." *Popular Mechanics*, October 1935.

Pope Meyer, Janice. "It Perks No More." *Indianapolis Courier-Journal Magazine*, April 24, 1960.

Reed, J. D. "Tacky Nostalgia? No, These Are Landmarks." *TIME*, December 11, 1989.

"Roadside Shops That Tourists Can't Overlook." *American Weekly*, November 8, 1936.

Rockefeller, Mrs. John D., Jr. "Small Wayside Refreshment Stand Competition." *Ladies' Home Journal*, November 1927.

Secter, Bob. "Upper Midwest Takes Stock in Fiberglass Fauna." *Los Angeles Times*, December 23, 1991.

Simon, Stephanie. "Metal Behemoths Punctuate Prairie Vistas in North Dakota." *Los Angeles Times*, August 24, 1999.

"Streamlined Diner." *Pacific Coast Record*, February 1941.

"Super Station Designed as Mosque." *National Petroleum News*, April 18, 1928.

Taylor, Frank. "Goodbye Harry Oliver." *Hollywood Studio Magazine*, September 1973.

"Teen Entrepreneur Turns Cool Profit with His Icy Cones." *Los Angeles Times*, October 11, 1983.

"Wandering Minstrel Rides Deluxe." *Los Angeles Times*, October 5, 1928.

"Weird Architecture Helps Sell Ice Cream." *Popular Mechanics*, January 1928.

Wiley, G. Harrison. "The House That Jack Builds." *The Motion Picture Director*, January 1926.

Wilson, Jane. "We Don't Know Where Ma Is, but We Got Pop on Ice." *West*, June 20, 1971.

"World's Queerest Eating Places." *Science and Invention*, April 1931.

## ACKNOWLEDGMENTS

When it comes to images and ideas, Benedikt Taschen is nonpareil in the world of publishing. He felt that this architectural category was one that should continue to be examined and celebrated, and it's through his support that this new volume exists. To that end, Mr. Taschen is to be applauded for recognizing the importance of all architectural types, be they high or low, while realizing that this specific type colorfully reflects the need to build structures that represent their time, place, and cultural attitudes.

Designer Ryan Mungia continues to steward the book process with precision and dexterity. Processing, organizing, and pulling each part together, he is the glue that binds this book and the other TASCHEN publications that we have worked together on for the past 18 years.

The editing, design, and production teams of TASCHEN are a well-oiled machine that can produce books with the highest of international standards. Together with our colleagues in Cologne—editor and project manager Jascha Kempe, graphic designer Tanja da Silva, prepress producer Tina Ciborowius, production manager Frank Goerhardt, and editorial director Mahros Allamezade, a perfect storm of collaboration was created in producing this book.

Archives and repositories of photographic imagery continue to provide the essential material for my and others' research. As guardians of these images they are key to the continuation of scholarly investigation for this project and previous iterations of *California Crazy*. Among the many institutions that were consulted for this and previous iterations of this project are the Los Angeles Public Library; San Diego History Center; San Francisco Public Library; University of California, Los Angeles; University of California, Santa Cruz; University of New Mexico; University of Southern California; and the Huntington Library.

To complete this new volume, I relied once again on the generosity and support of various individuals who lent material from their own collections. Rarely asking for compensation, they are satisfied knowing that their contributions advance and make visible histories that would evaporate without their participation. Many thanks to Laura Ackley, Steven Anaya, William Bradford, Genoa Caldwell, Victoria Daly, Donna Ewald Huggins, Alden Jewell, J. Eric Lynxwiler, Sandra Connolly McLain, Marc Wanamaker, Dan Watson, Greg Williams, and Tom Zimmerman.

The hunters and gatherers of the flea markets, swap meets, and ephemera shows who find obscure and rare treasures that otherwise would be lost to the dumpster of ignorance are the unsung heroes of scholarly research and the advancement of arcane knowledge. Rarely are they acknowledged for their craft and skills. Hats off to Jeff Bartholomew, Taylor Bowie, Ralph Bowman, Jeff Carr, Margo Essman, Mike Fairly, Gary Frederick, Gary Fredburg, Terre Hirsch, Bobby McDearmon, Robin Paeper, Greg Rivera, Eric Robbins, John Jacob Schram, Marc Selvaggio, Bruce Shyer, Terry Stroud, Doug Wayne, and Ben Ziegler, along with my scavenger buddies who have retired or are no longer with us: The Da Mamma's, Dan and Danny DePalma, Bob and Rhonda Heintz, and Buzz Kinnimont.

A special mention goes out to Leonard Lightfoot, whose impeccable taste and astute vision have turned up hundreds of rare and important images that have made their way into my collection.

Advocates for historic preservation, scholars, and the artists who continue to pursue the study of this architectural type are instrumental in keeping the California Crazy concept alive. Among them are Cristina Carbona, University of Louisville; the Los Angeles Conservancy and its dedicated members; Chris Nichols, who continues to be a major player in all things Los Angeles and also deserves to be bestowed the moniker of Mr. L.A.; Richard Gutman, whose devotion to the American diner paralleled my roadside interests; Marc Greuther of the Henry Ford Museum in Detroit, whose institutional acumen indemnifies the California Crazy subject as a serious and legitimate subject; and John Baeder, who has continued to support my passion for the past 50 years while never wavering from his own commitment to painting and collecting the American roadside.

Bobby Green, an entrepreneur who puts his money where his mouth is, should be the model for all of those developers who demolish our historic properties in the quest for lining their pockets with coin. He saw the value of saving the Idle Hour barrel in North Hollywood, envisioning it as a bar and café in its original condition as well as pristinely restoring the legendary Tail o' the Pup. He did it and he and his two partners, Dimitri Komarov and Dmitry Liberman, are reaping the rewards of successful historic preservation for those and their other projects.

Chris DeNoon, who is no longer with us, deserves a special mention as one of the original researchers on this subject matter in the 1970s and on many of my projects that ultimately became books. His enthusiasm never waned, and when little or no compensation was forthcoming, he still performed his job like a pro. This book and his own publications will serve as his legacy. His presence will always be felt in my future endeavors, and I will sorely miss him not only as a collaborator but as a dear friend of over 50 years.

Additionally, I would like to thank Blue Trimarchi and Brett Lund of Art Works for their premiere work and whose services I have employed and enjoyed for over 35 years.

Last but not least, a special thanks is reserved for Tyra Byers, who graciously permitted me to once again publish her father David Gebhard's landmark essay on programmatic architecture.

—Jim Heimann, Los Angeles

## CREDITS

All images are from the Jim Heimann Collection unless otherwise noted.

Steven Anaya Collection 43; Roger Beerworth 224; William Bradford 175 bottom; Bridgeman Images 432 top; John Hay Library, Brown University 431; Mott/Merge Collection, California History Room, California State Library, Sacramento, California 413, 414–415, 443; Culver City Chamber of Commerce 247 bottom; Victoria Daly 113 top, 192 bottom, 327; Bettmann/Getty Images 139; Hulton Archive/Getty Images 127 bottom, 432 bottom; The Burton Holmes Historical Collection 152, 189, 254 top, 270–271, 418; Photo by A. R. Hromatka courtesy of Alden Jewell 18–19; Donna Ewald Huggins 24, 26, 34; The Kobal Collection 39 bottom; Long Beach Public Library 377 top; Los Angeles Public Library 42, 216, 268 bottom, 276 bottom, 280, 310 bottom, 326 bottom, 354–355, 370 bottom; Ansel Adams, Ansel Adams Fortune Magazine Collection, Los Angeles Public Library 17 top, 326 top; Blackstock Negative Collection, Los Angeles Public Library 403; Eyre Powell Chamber of Commerce Collection, Los Angeles Public Library 227 top; Herald-Examiner Collection, Los Angeles Public Library 116 top; McAvoy-Torrence Historic Hollywood Collection, Los Angeles Public Library 148; Ralph Morris, Ralph Morris Collection, Los Angeles Public Library 40; Herman Schultheis, Herman J. Schultheis Collection, Los Angeles Public Library 171 top left, 232, 233, 269; Security Pacific National Bank Collection, Los Angeles Public Library 13 bottom, 15, 80, 83, 88 top, 106 bottom, 116–117, 131, 135 bottom, 162, 163 top and bottom, 187, 259 top and bottom, 268 top, 281, 278–279 top, 284, 285 left and right, 298–299, 304–305, 331 bottom, 334–335, 353, 357, 374–375, 384–385 top, 385 bottom, 394 bottom, 400, 422 bottom; John V. Twyman, Security Pacific National Bank Collection, Los Angeles, Public Library 58; Works Progress Administration Collection, Los Angeles Public Library 282–283, 307 top; J. Eric Lynxwiler Collection 78–79; Mike Connolly's Idle Hour Café, photo from the family collection of Sandra Connolly McLain 256 top and bottom; Ryan Mungia 470–471; J. Baylor Roberts, National Geographic Creative 149; San Diego History Center 275 top; San Francisco History Center, San Francisco Public Library 33 top and bottom, 27, 35, 37; The Seligman Family Foundation 32; Photo by Isaiah W. Tabler of Esquimaux Village, Souvenir of the California Midwinter International Exposition, BANC PIC 1976.029:70--ffALB. Bancroft Library, University of California, Berkeley 213; Courtesy Special Collections, UC Santa Cruz, Branson DeCou Archive 30–31; A&W Root Beer Stand, ca. 1950, 000-385. b3f42, Bainbridge Bunting Photograph Collection, PICT 000-385, Center for Southwest Research, University Libraries, University of New Mexico 449; University of Southern California 99 top, 138, 199, 307 bottom, 398–399 top, 426–427, 438; Photo by Dick Wittington courtesy of University of Southern California 9, 10–11, 12 bottom, 14 bottom, 16, 17 bottom, 98 bottom, 156 bottom, 158–159, 168–169 bottom; Marc Wanamaker Collection cover, 184–185, 392 top, 393 top,